BY THE SAME AUTHOR

Eighteenth Century Pastel Portraits (John Gifford Ltd., 1971)

NEW DAUGHTERS OF THE ORACLE

The Return of Female Prophetic Power in Our Time

Virginia Adair

New Paradigm Books Boca Raton   2001

NEW PARADIGM BOOKS
<http://www.newpara.com>
22783 South State Road 7, Suite 97
Boca Raton, FL 33428
Tel.: (561) 482-5971, FAX: (561) 852-8322
E-mail: <jdc@flinet.com>

A first, slightly different, edition of this book was published as *Women of a Higher Nature*, by Alexander Associates, of Cornwall, England, in 1999, ISBN Number 1 899526 16 1, Library of Congress Catalog Card Number 99-60393.

New Daughters of the Oracle:
The Return of Female Prophetic Power in Our Time
By Virginia Adair
Copyright © 2001 Virginia Adair

Cover nebula photo courtesy of NASA/JPL/CalTech

Cover design by Peri Poloni, Knockout Design
<http://www.knockoutbooks.com>
2584 Greenwood Lane, Suite 11
Cameron Park, CA 95682
E-mail: <peri@knockoutbooks.com>

First New Paradigm Books Quality Paperback Edition, June 15, 2001
New Paradigm Books ISBN Number: 1-892138-03-4
Library of Congress Control Number: 00-135257

10 9 8 7 6 5 4 3 2 1

oracle n. **1.** A shrine consecrated to the worship and consultation of a prophetic god, such as that of Apollo at Delphi. **2.** The priest or other transmitter of prophecies at such a shrine. **3.** A prophecy made known at such a shrine, often in the form of an enigmatic statement or allegory. **4.** Any person or agency considered to be a source of wise counsel or prophetic opinions; an infallible authority or judge.

- *The American Heritage Dictionary of the English Language*

TABLE OF CONTENTS

NEW DAUGHTERS OF THE ORACLE

The Return of Female Prophetic Power
in Our Time

Illustration.   The Author Among the *Dukins* of Bali   Facing page 1

Bali, Indonesia: The author (*left*) speaks through an inter-preter (*right*) with Ibu Wayan Ginada, *dukin*, or witchdoctor

(Chapter 32. Bali, Indonesia: Witchcraft Among the *Dukins*)

Introduction

The Psychic Gift:
Throwback, or Leap Forward?

In Bergen County, New Jersey, in the late 1970s, a ghastly series of murders took place. The circumstances of each slaying were so similar that a single assailant was thought to be responsible. A concerted manhunt was underway when still another young woman in the area disappeared. The police, fearing she might be the killer's latest victim, mounted an even more desperate search. The papers ran photos of the young woman, in hopes someone had seen her or could provide a lead as to her whereabouts.

A clairvoyant named Joy Herald happened to read an account of the disappearance. As she studied the accompanying photo of the woman, she suddenly 'saw' water, and then, less distinctly, a very tall man. She went to the police and told them of her vision; they happened to mention that one of the locations targeted for possible search was an area called Tallman Park.

"That's it!" Joy exclaimed. "It's not a tall man. It's the lake in Tallman Park. That's what this vision is trying to tell me!"

The police dragged the lake in Tallman Park. In its quiet depths, they found the slain body of the missing woman.

When we meet Joy Herald later in this book, we will learn how her subsequent visions trapped the psychotic killer and led to his arrest, thus ending a nightmare of fear for the citizens of Bergen County.

Does a valuable gift like Joy's contain intimations of a new direction in mankind's evolution? If there is even the remote possibility that this might be the case, scientists and anthropologists the world over should be studying minds like hers.

For centuries the curious have asked, Is intuition—the sixth sense—a residual trait from an earlier stage in mankind's evolution, which crops up now and then like a recessive gene, with women seemingly experiencing it more—or denying it less? Or, have these

1

intuitive flashes always been heralds of a more advanced direction that our species may one day be destined to take?

To put it another way: Was a sixth sense present in the mind of early man, helping him to survive as he emerged from brute instinct to rational thought, and then receding as that intuitive sense became less necessary? Or might such a faculty be a relatively new mechanism for accessing our brain's potential, one which will one day cause us to redefine what it means to be a human?

If we agree with the geneticists that evolution is an ongoing process and that we can influence its course, then the thoughts of contemporary philosopher Kent B. Van Cleave bear repeating. Mr. Van Cleave asserts that evolution is prompted by three specific needs: the need for security, the need for variety, and the need for excellence.

The first need, that of security, is essential, he says, so that that which is new may dare to venture forth.

Perhaps the wave of humanism which peaked in the Renaissance of the fourteenth to sixteenth centuries—and which was characterized by a focus on the natural abilities of man rather than on the powers of the supernatural—frightened this fledgling mutation of a sixth sense back into its hiding place. The humbled and frightened seers of the time were lumped together with the frauds, the ignorantly superstitious, the insane; persons with genuine powers of healing or clairvoyance were denigrated and denounced. Of that period, psychiatrist Gregory Zelboorg has written, "the differentiation among a mentally sick person, a witch, [and] a heretic became less and less definite, so that toward the middle of the thirteenth century these became synonymous in the mind of man."

Since it is generally believed that evolution is ever continuing, sometimes slowly, sometimes in quantum leaps, is it too much to believe then that the renewed interest in psychic phenomena so prevalent in the lay world today may be an unconscious realization on the part of our species that evolution is building up to another one of those giant leaps forward? If this is indeed the case, then by now we should be using the evaluative tools of modern science to rule out the fraudulent and to identify and celebrate those rare individuals whose claims to psychic power are legitimate. Those possessing proven paranormal gifts should no longer be treated with skepticism and ridicule, for if they are they will be driven once again into the shadows.

The gifts of the painter, the writer, the musician, are praised and envied; all too often the psychic, because of his or her special gifts, is treated by many as a social pariah—a mere curiosity at best, an object of fear at worst. For the most part, psychics are still passed off as charlatans and fakes. But isn't there a great deal which pretends to be art and literature which is actually totally valueless? We easily accept this latter sort of fakery without a universal condemnation of painters and writers; why do we not extend the same courtesy to psychics?

Those who actually do have psychic powers, powers beyond the normal, deserve our protection and respect. Yet I often fear that in our time they will meet the same fate as that which was usually meted out to their forebears in the Middle Ages and the Renaissance. All too vulnerable to being tarred by the same brush as tars contemporary fads such as commercialized "channeling," syndicated "psychic prediction," and hysterical "healing," those rare individuals who really do see beyond our own time and place, whose minds do indeed comprehend another dimension, are once more in danger of being discredited or ignored.

In the Boston Mensa's magazine, *Beacon,* Martha Morelock told a revealing fable. It concerned people, living together in a community, who were very much alike. One woman living among them was different; she had odd objects on her face that allowed her to sense certain impressions that the others were unable to perceive. In the end, those others became so frightened by her extrasensory powers, which they couldn't explain, that they banded together and killed the woman. We then learn that, of course, the strange objects on the woman's face were eyes, and those who had discredited her, and then killed her...were blind.

It is the case that, in every discipline, what is obscure to some is clear to others. For a true psychic, knowing the future is quite normal—just as *not* knowing the future is quite normal for the vast majority of us. Imagine that you are looking at a portrait of Marie Antoinette as a happy young school girl, or at a photograph of a nation's president when he is still a callow schoolboy. "Ah," you're able to say, gazing at these pictures, "I know what's in store for you!" Perhaps, for the true clairvoyant, it is all "there" in much the same way when he or she gazes at a client. For the true clairvoyant, time does not run in a straight line from the past to the future.

What makes the "knowing" of the psychic—or of the oracle, he or she who foretells the future—even less understandable or acceptable to us is that it functions as something of a random faculty, not necessarily available on demand. It is conceivable that, as man evolved, the first feeble flutterings of the faculty of reason may also have been random and faulty; fortunately for us, there was no one around to discourage its development.

The term *psi* may be defined as the aggregate of parapsychological functions of the mind, including extrasensory perception, precognition (foreseeing the future), and psychokinesis (mentally causing physical changes). The fact that these functions manifest themselves in ways that are usually random, elusive, and unpredictable, demands that the very finest scientific minds address this subject. In the hard sciences, there are ways to identify charlatans and frauds; there are checks and controls to keep the scientific fraternity relatively free of impostors. But, in the realm of the psychic, things are not so black and white, and anyone can make claims which are difficult to prove or to refute. The great English philosopher David Hume commented on the stigma which in his time still attached to all psychic phenomena; that stigma still exists today, despite the widespread influence of the so-called 'New Age.' In the words of British psychologist Susan Blackmore, "psychic research has failed to establish itself as a respectable area of scientific inquiry."

But every church, synagogue, cathedral, temple and mosque throughout the world is a monument to man's abiding belief in something beyond the phenomena perceived by the five senses. The reverence and respect paid to the oracles and sibyls of ancient times, to the early prophets of the Judeo-Christian era, to the Enlightened Ones of the Far East, bear witness to man's perennial belief in the existence of a sixth sense. Why then do scientists turn away, without at least taking a closer look?

There *are* people living among us today who can sometimes 'see' into the past and future. There *are* people living among us today who can manifest at times the gift of healing. Scientists should accept this fact, then set about developing methodologies by which these rare beings can be identified and separated out in our thinking from the frauds; the scientific community should study and encourage the workings of the remarkable brains of these persons. Those individuals who are gifted psychically need to be rescued from the "fantastic kitchen of vulgar charlatans," as it was so vividly described over a hundred years ago by French occultist Oswald Wirth in *L'Imposition Des Mains Dans La Médecine Philosophile [The Laying-On of Hands in Philosophical Medicine]*. Those who try to exploit the occult for greedy purposes have always existed, and still exist today; but, by now, we should be able to develop the means to weed them out. Our ablest minds need to be at work sorting out the real from the bogus.

Having unlocked so many of life's mysteries—having contributed immeasurably to the health and happiness of mankind—scientists are today the ones to whom we naturally turn. It is they who in this age are the acknowledged judges and jurors; it is they who should be making an unbiased effort to tackle the fascinating mystery of *psi*—but, first, they must be convinced that *psi* exists. Those scientific disciplines that reduce all phenomena to a materialistic basis may in fact not be adequate to a full understanding of the nature of reality; a totally different approach may be required.

There appear to be three types of persons who display an appreciative interest in the paranormal. The first is the person who maintains a nagging doubt that the world as experienced by the five senses is "all that there really is." No matter how rewarding and pleasurable the particular lives of such persons may be, they always have the vague feeling that they are not in the main tent, but merely in an anteroom, while the real show is unfolding somewhere else. Even without flashes of so-called "cosmic consciousness," even with their attention focused entirely on the practical, such persons can never savor their success to the fullest nor accept unquestioningly their privileged place in society, so long as other people are suffering or if they themselves can in the end only look forward to oblivion. The meaning of it all eludes them; they keenly feel that pieces of the puzzle must be missing, that something must be going on behind the scenes that they're not privy to.

The second type of person who pursues the unexplained with interest are those who have little sense of self, who feel they have but little control over their lives and who are forever searching for some outside, unseen element or influence which is responsible for the direction of their fates. These are the ones, of course, who are most likely to fall prey to the frauds and charlatans flooding the arena.

The third group are those who are justifiably curious about that which they cannot understand. I recall an old-world Austrian, impeccable beyond describing, an absolute exemplar of decorum and taste, and of whom it was said that he had only a single fault: he was curious about "those dirty old gypsies who can see the future." Now, the gypsies might have been old, and they might have been dirty, but why fault the venerable count for his wonder at their paranormal powers? We should all periodically examine our attitudes and our prejudices.

Greta Woodrew, an astonishing woman whom you will meet later, recounts an experience which sadly illustrates the level of esteem attaching to clairvoyants. Greta once received an urgent call from a Washington senator who, without giving his name, asked her quickly if she might be able to help him find a valuable heirloom pin his wife had recently lost. In her book *Memories of Tomorrow*, Greta tells the story:

I'd never located a missing object over the telephone before, but something told me to ask if his wife did any gardening. He allowed this was true...
"Has she planted any pansies lately?"
"She has a gorgeous pansy garden," he affirmed.

"Tell her to go look near the little pansy faces, and I believe she will find her pin lying there."

Sounding excited, the senator said he would run outside and check. When he returned, he was so elated I could hardly understand what he was saying. "It's in my hand!" he shouted. "It was just where you said! This is amazing! It's absolutely amazing!"

Naturally, I was pleased to have been of service, and, figuring that he owed me rather more information than he had given me at the start, I said, "Now senator, would you tell me your name?"

The excitement abruptly left his voice, which now sounded quite horrified. "Oh no!" he said. "I'm grateful, of course, but I can't afford to take the risk of having any of my constituents finding out that I consulted a psychic. You understand, it's so—so...flaky!" And, so saying, he hung up.

We feel no embarrassment in admitting that we have talked about our problems to a lawyer, or a tax accountant, or a financial consultant. Yet, is their intellectual judgment always infallibly correct? Instead of characterizing Greta's gift as "flaky," the senator should have immediately set in motion a bill providing government funding for a study of minds such as hers.

Chapter 1

Rome, Italy; and Beyond:
The Pain of Signora Giardini Plants a Seed

- *"Io vedo tanta tristezza ogni giorno, senza il poter avertirlo."*
- *"I see so much sadness every day, without the power to avert it."*

From childhood I have harbored three quite unrelated obsessions: a love of eighteenth century portraiture, an unrelenting curiosity about faraway places, and a powerful—if often ambivalent—fascination with the paranormal.

Fortunately, I have been able to satisfy all three of these obsessions. I myself pursued a career as a portrait painter in the classical tradition, and, at the close of World War II, married someone who shared my love of travel and whose career as head of international operations for a large American company took us and our growing family to lengthy postings in South America and Europe, with frequent trips to the Middle East, Africa, and the Orient.

During much of this time, my interest in the paranormal remained unsatisfied, hovering tantalizingly on the periphery of my thoughts, never explained, never resolved—almost an annoyance. What if the things one heard <u>were</u> true?

Some years ago, my ambivalence concerning the subject was finally resolved. This came about as the result of a visit I paid to a certain Signora Giardini, who—like ourselves— was living in Rome at the time. Signora Giardini's reputation had become firmly established when word got around that she had—or at least so went the rumor—warned World War II Italian dictator Benito Mussolini that he would one day hang by his heels. This prediction, of course, became a reality, when Mussolini was literally strung up by the heels by Italian partisans in the closing months of the war. How, I asked myself, when I first heard this story, could Signora Giardini have possibly known? The details of Mussolini's death were so unusual! Could it have been simply a lucky guess? Or is there <u>actually</u> such a thing as psychic ability?

The Return of Female Prophetic Power in Our Time

I remember that long ago day when I decided to visit Signora Giardini myself—a day that would mark, however subtly, a turning point in my life. I remember vividly our meeting and the curious prediction with which it ended.

It was February; the skies over Rome were bleak and glowering and the chill in the damp air penetrated to the very bone. It was the kind of day that innocent people use for innocent pursuits, such as staying indoors and sorting through old photographs, or answering the letters of long-neglected friends.

I was feeling just a little guilty, though, as I raced through the damp streets, as I spent an hour waiting in the dimly-lit anteroom of Signora Giardini's *atelier*, or studio, and as I finally took my place in front of the Signora's crystal ball. I confess that I had come in part out of idle curiosity, having always felt that "fortunetellers" (as I mentally categorized them) were somehow suspect and that the people who consulted them were abdicating all responsibility for their destiny in so doing.

I had to admit that my thoughts on the abdication of personal responsibility might simply have been a negative comment only on the persons consulting the fortuneteller, and not on the fortuneteller herself. I did wonder why the seers, who have proven their ability to foretell the future, are so often and so casually demeaned. Was it because we need to dismiss what we can't understand? The day I arrived at Signora Giardini's, I had just about decided that such judgements might perhaps be a form of xenophobia, or a fear of the unknown. For the fact is that psychics, oracles and the like make us feel vaguely uncomfortable. Their gifts upset too many of our firmly held beliefs and too many of our ego-satisfying assumptions. We find it less threatening to patronizingly dismiss them altogether—instead of treating them with the respect that they deserve. All in all, it seemed to me that far too much of this tantalizing phenomenon was being written off as unworthy of serious study.

It was in this frame of mind that I found myself seated in the Signora's inner sanctum, as it were, on that bleak and gloomy Roman afternoon, and gazing across the crystal ball at her intense

9

face. And I must admit this: that, from the first moment I set eyes on her, I had felt—oddly, almost inexplicably—a great tide of sympathy rising in me for this total stranger. I'd been told her highly conservative family was deeply embarrassed by her interest in the metaphysical, so much so that they had cut themselves off from her. Whether this was true or not, I had no way of knowing. She was still tall and erect, with her dark hair combed severely back from her finely chiseled features. Her mouth was unsmiling, and, more than that, her deep-set eyes reflected the profoundest sadness and resignation. She seemed too weary even to want to speak. Later, just before the end of our session, she would tell me that she considered her gift an almost intolerable burden: "*Io vedo tanta tristezza ogni giorno, senza il poter avertirlo,*" she would utter, groaning, "I see so much sadness every day, without the power to avert it." But, by that point, my sympathy for her had swelled to such a degree that, when she pronounced these words, I simply felt myself fortunate indeed to be in the presence of a mind that could demonstrate such powers, and certainly ones that mine could not.

At the end of the sitting, I was allowed one question. "Do I have anything new to say to the world?" I asked her, with the breathless missionary zeal of youth.

The signora gave a heavy sigh. She placed her hands on the crystal ball, closed her large sad eyes, and slowly shook her head.

The answer seemed to be, "No."

And then, in a barely audible voice, Signora Giardini murmured something further. I strained to hear the words she added; they were: "But, wait, perhaps, perhaps...someday...someday to the very young."

That was the end of the session. I would never see her again.

Yes, that day was indeed a turning point in my life. I carefully filed Signora Giardini's prediction away in my memory. Over the next few years, my wonderment persisted—and, indeed, only increased—regarding those who say they can read the past, or tell the future, or mentally heal the sick. From that day on, I paid the closest attention to any account of a paranormal event. I read book after book on psychic phenomena. It seemed to me that if even a single one of the claims was valid, that claim was worth serious study —for its implications were enormous.

Though when my husband retired we returned to our native Atlanta, we decided to continue the worldwide travel we both so enjoyed. This, I realized, would give me an opportunity to talk to people in a variety of circumstances and in a diversity of cultures— people who allegedly demonstrated psychic abilities. Assuming the sixth sense appears more often in women than in men—or is less denied by them—I decided to limit my search to women, not unmindful of the fact that, in ancient times, it was mainly women who were the oracles and sibyls through whom the gods were said to utter prophetic words. Could the daughters of these oracles, so to speak, have survived into modern times? Could they, indeed, still be flourishing? The time had come for me to satisfy a lifelong curiosity. Postponement was no longer an option.

As 'random' appears to be the operative word in manifestations of *psi*, these women would be chosen randomly. I would hear of several in an area and randomly choose one to seek out. I soon found that their manifestations of the sixth sense differed as much as their individual backgrounds—and yet, as you will see, that there were startling similarities in their personal histories.

This book is a result of those travels. I came across far stranger paranormal phenomena than I could ever have imagined, from far more sources of unimpeachable integrity than I could ever have expected. Hopefully, some very young scientist will read of them in this book and see them as a challenge, and with his knowledge and technical tools seek to discover the principles involved.

In any event, as I started out on this unusual quest I was trusting in Signora Giardini's prediction; I was acting as if that "someday" had finally arrived.

Chapter 2

Shipton-under-Wychwood, England:
Learning the Language of Pendulums

My quest began not without certain misgivings. I'd often heard that hearing voices and seeing visions were symptoms of insanity. I wondered how I would be able to draw the line between clairaudience, clairvoyance, and madness.

In this regard, there came to my mind a certain Hungarian hostess whom I'd known in Madrid, who could well serve as an example. Tall and imposing in appearance, she had given a succession of *soirées* every spring in her well-appointed flat near El Retiro park. A notorious wit had once put it about that her guest list read like a roundup of would-be dropouts from the *Almanach de Gotha*. She did seem to surround herself with lots of black sheep, indigents, and ne'er-do-wells culled from certain noble houses of Europe—or such as were drifting in and out of Spain in the 1960s and could reluctantly be cornered.

All that was required for an invitation on those evenings when she "received" was an ancient name and, hopefully, a slim figure. She felt the fat were socially incorrect; they ate too much, were a threat to the chairs, and tended to have damp foreheads. Of course, royalty in exile, or its blood kinsmen however far removed, could be forgiven anything. But these were hard to snare and seldom returned a second time, since they were sure to find at her receptions the very people they spent their lifetimes trying to avoid.

After a particularly heady evening during which no less than three ex-ambassadors and a well-known bullfighter put in a brief appearance, our hostess, who by her own admission had stayed up far too late and drunk far too many magnums of champagne, finally retired in complete exhaustion. The following morning, she insisted that the furniture had been moved around in her drawing room. She also claimed that a painting had mysteriously disappeared from the wall.

And then, there were the "voices."

This marked the beginning of her long slow descent into madness. There were those who said she should have been taken seriously in her intuitions; that perhaps indeed "poltergeists could have been at work." But her defenders, alas, were as likely to have had a history of instability themselves. In the end, the Hungarian hostess had been placed by her family in a clinic for the mentally deranged, even though many of her friends still staunchly maintained that she was sane.

I fully realized what I was up against. There would be no road signs on my quest, no established facts. I was on my own.

Sometimes in the summers I go to England, to our small flat in an old country house in the village of Shipton-under-Wychwood. The Wychwood Forest, once the hunting reserve of medieval kings, lies to the north, while to the west lies the village of Burford with its ancient stone houses and its timeworn Gothic church. Such legend-filled surroundings, such a region thick with ghosts of the past, was not too unlikely a spot, I'm sure you'll agree, from which to start the kind of search I was embarking on.

You hear things in a village. People have a way of knowing about the presence of the supernormal, and of passing the word along. Certain rumors had reached my ears, and that was why, on a damp July evening, I found myself standing at the entrance to a small plaster-and-frame cottage lying opposite Coombs Close. The cottage was protected by tall hedges which lined the road, while a militant row of rain-washed hollyhocks stood sentinel along the footpath leading to the door; it was the birthplace and present home of Irma Coombs Williams.

I was quickly ushered into a dark, narrow sitting room whose proportions seemed to shrink even more when the tall, imposing figure of Irma Coombs Williams rose to greet me. My hostess had a very distinctive presence. Her dark riveting eyes were rendered even more piercing by the straight white hair which framed her square-set features; you felt a great energy flowing from this person. Mrs. Williams was known throughout the village as a highly intelligent woman who could cure allergies through diet. What

13

was particularly interesting to me was that these cures were individually arrived at by the use of a small wooden pendulum!

I was glad that pendulums were not really all that bizarre; it had been best, I'd thought, not to start off with anything too startling. The art of dowsing has been around for a long time, and today even the most skeptical grant it a certain measure of grudging acceptance.

When we'd gotten past the introductory banalities —"Won't you sit down?" — "Such an unusually chilly summer." — "How kind of you to let me come!" — I broached the subject of her reputed successes with the pendulum. Mrs. Williams replied in a tone of voice that established her authority immediately. "I dowse for health!" she proclaimed firmly, looking me straight in the eye.

I asked her to explain.

"Well, if one man's meat is another man's poison, then we need to know what our own particular dietary requirements are. Not only what we require, but what we should avoid."

I nodded in agreement. She continued: "Do you realize that in your United States alone, over 40 million people are known to have some form of allergy? I imagine that here in England the percentage is not likely to be very different. Add to this shocking statistic the many undiagnosed instances of physical and psychological *malaise* which in actual fact are caused by food sensitivities; many people who are labeled as 'hypochondriacs' or even as 'neurotics' have found that a change of diet can change their lives!"

Irma Coombs Williams was now totally absorbed in her subject. Though I could guess what her answer would be, I still asked her, "And how does one arrive at one's own optimum diet?"

"By using a pendulum. It is really quite easy. The pendulum offers a way of tuning into the subconscious and tapping the reservoir of knowledge stored there."

Before I could ask another question, she hastened to explain. "The pendulum can help make this knowledge available to us at all times, if we use it properly. There are electromagnetic energies from substances—food, drink, and so forth, and, of course, from ourselves. The pendulum picks up the interaction of these energies, how one affects the other. I believe it was Albert Einstein who first suggested that dowsing relies on electromagnetic energies. The movements of the pendulum are subconsciously motivated. Our fingers carry enough information and respond enough to the items being tested to set the pendulum in motion. Whether a substance is beneficial, and by how much, can be conveyed by the different movements of the pendulum and by the vigor of these movements. Do you understand?"

I was greatly impressed. "Can anyone dowse?" I asked.

"Well, I would say one person in three is able to dowse immediately, and an equal number probably could in time become proficient with practice. There are some people, however, who cannot seem to dowse at all." At my look of surprise, she went on to explain that, "Tension, drugs, the misalignment of bones in the neck which can cause pressure in one of the meridians, as they are called by acupuncturists—any one of these factors can leave the pendulum totally dead."

Lest I should believe that dowsing for health was a simple matter, Irma Coombs Williams hastened to add: "No dowsing result can ever be considered final. Remember that. The needs of the body can change from one day to the next and even from one meal to the next, particularly for the hypersensitive person. I have known some unfortunate 'allergics' who were forced to dowse every item at every meal!"

She countered my look of disbelief by raising her eyebrows and declaring: "Better that, certainly, than gasping for breath, than swollen eyes, than itching and burning skin—." The mere thought of such indignities made me quickly agree.

All the time she was speaking, my eyes kept straying to the small wooden object I glimpsed every time she opened her hand to emphasize a point. "The pendulum is a very personal instrument," she was now saying. "It works for one person at one length of thread, at a different length of thread for another." Having finished her explanation, she finally loosened her grip on the small wooden object shaped like a child's elongated top that she held in her hand, and let it drop the full length of the thread to which it was attached.

Irma Coombs Williams stood up in a businesslike manner to show me how to hold the thread and how to find the best length at which to suspend the pendulum. "Dowsing should always be done over a plain wooden surface," she explained. "And never use metal to hold the item being tested; use only glass or china."

Seating herself once more beside me at a table, she continued: "When you dowse, let your elbow rest on the table, and place the pendulum over one substance at a time, until you have learned your pendulum's language."

"My pendulum's language?"

"Yes. A pendulum's language can vary from one person to another. Generally though, a clockwise rotation represents a 'building up' substance—one that is building health in the body—while an anti-clockwise rotation indicates a cleansing substance which may or may not be totally good for you. A back-and-forth swing usually suggests an adverse or allergic response to a substance—one that should be avoided altogether. A sidewise swing may indicate a substance neither particularly good nor particularly bad. However, you must remember that we are not all polarized the same way, so that for some people the clockwise and anti-clockwise rotation is reversed. There are even those who reverse the swing movements so that sidewise, rather than back-and-forth, indicates an allergic reaction. Interestingly enough, certain people find that their pendulums have only two main movements, clockwise indicating good, and anti-clockwise indicating bad. So you see, it is only by practice that you can learn what your pendulum is saying to you."

Before I could ask another question, Irma Coombs Williams had crossed the floor and disappeared through the entrance to a narrow hall. Moments later she returned, carrying a small wooden tray upon which lay a carrot, an apple, and a sugar bowl.

"Now, put your arm here on the table," she said. I did as I was told. She steadied her elbow on the opposite side of the table, grasped the string several inches above the pendulum, and dangled it over my arm. I assumed she must be picking up electromagnetic energies. She then held the pendulum a few inches above the sugar bowl. In just seconds, the little wooden pendulum began to swing vigorously back and forth; it was delivering its dread verdict.

The demonstration went on for about 30 minutes, with many more items being conveyed up the hallway from the pantry. As mesmerizing as I found all this, the hour was getting late, and there was much more I wanted to learn about this tall, statuesque woman who had lived all her life in this remote little village in Oxfordshire. The ability to dowse certainly seemed to be a manifestation of the paranormal; still, I ventured to ask her, "Aside from the pendulum, do you have any sorts of psychic illuminations?"

Her big dark eyes narrowed as she regarded me in silence.

She was probably wondering if I'd be able to understand. I have come to realize that many clairvoyants hesitate to talk about their visions for fear they will be ridiculed, or that these visions, if articulated in everyday terms, will lose much of their meaning. In any event, Irma Coombs Williams decided to take that risk, and she began to speak in a quiet, assured voice:

"Yes, I have illuminations. They come quite unexpectedly, following long periods of meditation, and are preceded by sharp, cramp-like sensations in the region of my solar plexus."

"What sorts of illuminations?" I asked.

"They usually come in the form of answers to questions which have been troubling me, namely, questions concerning healing and the organization of matter. After an illumination has come to me, a book often turns up, frequently within hours of the illumination, to verify its contents or to clarify it. Books will appear totally unexpectedly. The coincidences have been staggering.

"There were times, too, when the books themselves became the trigger for some of the phenomena I experienced." Her voice had become almost a whisper. "Once, when I was reading, the answer to the question of how it is possible for some people to know the future or pick up the past suddenly surfaced. A few days later, part two of this problem was triggered by another book, and a detailed description of how the answer could be represented on a piece of paper, rather as if it were a geometric pattern, became quite clear. Now, shall I tell you about the most remarkable and beautiful experience of this kind that I ever had?"

Before I could answer, she went on, her eyes growing luminous as she spoke. "One afternoon, at a time when I had been eager to understand the phenomenon of the 'group soul,' I was reading a book on a totally different subject when my eyes caught sight of the word 'c-e-l-l,' *cell*, in the text. It was then that my illumination occurred. It unfurled from left to right, rather as a scroll does, and yet I was also aware of perceiving it as a whole. I felt as though I were witnessing the scene from the outside, but at the same time experiencing it as a participant. Such double perception has always been a hallmark of extended consciousness, you know.

"In my 'group soul' illumination, I was shown a single cell—the first cell of life. Then the picture unscrolled to show how this single cell had led to other cells, then to show them continually joining together to form higher and higher forms of life, right on through the entire course of evolution until mankind was reached. Then there appeared in the middle of the scroll a vertical black line, and I knew that this was the death line—the division between the world of the body and the world of the spirit.

"The vision continued to unfold on the other side of the line, and it was almost an exact replica of what had unfolded on the first side. A cell—the 'soul cell,' if you like—appeared, and was joined by others. And, as before, each joining produced a higher organism, though this time it was actually a group organism; nevertheless, the souls were so joined in aspiration and purpose as to become in essence one body. By this joining together, they became stronger, wiser and more able to perform the tasks allotted to them. This aggregation of souls into groups of higher and higher consciousness continued to unscroll to the far right of my vision, until it finally disappeared from view."

She closed her eyes for a moment.

"Here, my illumination ended. I was left wondering if the aggregation of soul cells had become a part of God, their energy renewing His, or whether the whole cycle, from the first cell of physical life onward, was about to begin all over again. I realized that I—no one—would ever know the answer." She clasped her large capable hands together. "It was a great and glorious experience, one which will remain clearly with me for the rest of my life!"

We sat quietly for a minute. Irma Coombs Williams broke the silence. "One cannot experience psychic/mystical phenomena without being quite deeply affected. In my case, this illumination turned my understanding of the world upside-down."

Soon, we said good-bye. As I stepped out into the warm rain, she placed a small wooden pendulum in my hand. As I left her, she called out after me:

"Be careful. The nights are quite dark in the village."

It was almost a warning to be careful in my quest.

Hurrying home through the chilling mist, I thought about the effect of food on the brain and about the frequent admonitions to fast which are found in so many of the world's religions. Perhaps, it occurred to me, these admonitions have little to do with self-denial or sacrifice, but stem rather from the knowledge that food can affect the brain in unpredictable ways. At the extreme, we've long accepted the fact that certain foods can trigger highly bizarre behavior in persons who are particularly sensitive to some component of those foods. Perhaps fasting is practiced so as to eliminate any possibility of a food's affecting the thought processes, at those times when one wishes the channels to be kept clear to receive spiritual inspiration.

Chapter 3

London, England: Jasmin and the Return of Female Prophetic Power

The following morning, I drove down the motorway to London, heading through the Sunday traffic to an address I'd been told I might perhaps find useful. Just beyond the Victoria and Albert Museum, there's Queen's Park, and just off to the left Queensbury Street, which houses the College of Psychic Studies and the vast library of esoterica that it contains.

It was here that I met with Marie McDonald Cheerie, a medium and teacher of psychic development. There was a fresh wholesomeness about Marie's appearance; her eyes were bright blue, her smile engaging. Nothing about her hinted at seances, at tapping tables, at mysterious spirits—at any of the paraphrenalia the word "mediumship" usually connotes. Instead, Marie McDonald Cheerie struck me as someone who perhaps baked her own bread or gave piano lessons to the neighbors' children on Saturday mornings. My quest would be filled with many such surprises—and, in this case, with a good bit of good fortune; Marie was in London only for that day, which would save me the lengthy trip to her home in Cornwall.

"When did it all begin," I asked her, "the realization that you possessed an unusual gift?"

"I wasn't aware it was unusual," she told me. "Like so many little girls, I had imaginary playmates. But I could actually 'see' mine." Marie flashed her quick warm smile. "But I did not have a happy childhood." The smile faded quickly. "My mother died when I was quite young, and so I had to take care of the house for my father and look after my younger brother. I was married at 18. A few years later, my grandmother died. She had always been my mainstay."

Marie's voice broke. "My grandmother died in the most brutal way: She was murdered. This was doubly dreadful because the crime was committed by a neighbour, a young boy whom we'd always known and always been fond of. He must have been in some sort of trouble, and needed money. He was trying to rob her, and then—." Marie's voice broke again. She resumed with difficulty: "After that, everything seemed to change. My younger brother began to drink heavily. I became terribly depressed. Somehow, all my sensations became markedly heightened. I felt I couldn't cope anymore.

"Strangely enough, through all of this I was constantly aware of my grandmother's presence. But I could never be quite comforted by her presence, because of the cruel way that she had died.

"It was at about this time that I began to have psychic illuminations, vivid premonitions of random events—usually highly unpleasant ones, I might add. My feelings about myself became painfully confused. My husband thought I might find some explanation or comfort by visiting a medium. I'd been brought up in the Catholic Church, so at first I hesitated. Finally, in hopes of resolving some of my doubts about life and death, I reluctantly agreed to attend a seance. It was called a 'developmental group,' and it was led by a well-known trance-medium.

"Two strange incidents took place during my first visit. The first was that a member of the group pointed in my direction, then pointed at the medium, then shouted loudly, 'She's like you!' This odd outburst over, we all sat quietly and meditated. Then, as we were saying a prayer, a feeling of panic and suffocation suddenly seized me. I ran from the room in terror, vowing never to return.

"Some days later, persuaded by my husband, I went back for another session. This time, while I was sitting in a circle with the other members, my eyes became fixated on the electric wall heater. The light from this electric wall heater quickly became a source of great annoyance to me. At the same time, it served as a sort of hypnotic focal point, which I seemed unable to resist. A member of the group sprang up to turn it off—and, at that very moment, I slipped into a deep trance.

"As for the events that followed, I can only relate what was later told me, for I remembered nothing myself. According to those present, the apparition of a Japanese girl entered the circle. The medium revealed that she was not surprised, since she had been told this girl was coming. The apparition gave her name as Jasmin. She went around the circle quickly, giving each of us a personally significant message; it was as if she were establishing her credibility.

"Finally, she came to me, and said that she had chosen me 'through whom to speak.' Jasmin explained that, to further her own spiritual growth, she had elected to become a 'spirit guide' in order to help those who were still on earth."

As I was listening closely to Marie, it had struck me that this was rather like what was done by the *boddhisattvas* of the Buddhists, those enlightened beings who are said to refuse *nirvana*, preferring to reincarnate one more time on earth and act as guides to humanity. But on the whole I found Marie's story difficult to accept. I ventured to ask her if perhaps the voice of Jasmin might not simply have been a product of her own thoughts.

"Oh, I wondered that for a long time myself," she answered, "and so did my husband, who is always a great skeptic. We needed to be certain Jasmin was a separate entity. So you can imagine how pleased I was when a well-known doctor who taught at Oxford's Balliol College heard about my mediumship, became interested, and proposed to carry out certain tests on me. He wanted to see if he would actually be able to speak to Jasmin himself. I agreed to go into trance for this purpose and to let Jasmin take over my mind and body."

I leaned forward so I wouldn't miss a word. Marie began:

"It happened that the Oxford don was Chinese, but he had neglected to tell me that he planned to question Jasmin in Mandarin—a major Chinese dialect I have no knowledge of whatsoever. The interview was taped while I was in deep trance. I learned about what transpired only after I returned to normal consciousness.

"I was told that Jasmin had given correct answers to all the professor's questions, which she had understood perfectly; but that she had said she preferred to give the answers in English, explaining that her vocal chords were not trained to the variations of pitch

22

necessary to make herself well understood in Chinese. Midway through the session, the Oxford doctor had switched to Cantonese and to various other dialects of Chinese, each of which Jasmin had been able to understand, though she admonished him to, 'Stop playing games with me!'

"Finally, the eminent don—who was also a scholar in Far Eastern affairs—questioned Jasmin about ancient Japanese mythology, again an area which I've never studied. Yet the answers Jasmin gave were always correct. Then he asked Jasmin questions about little-known locations in Japan, and here, too, she unfailingly gave the correct answer.

"The questioning went on for three hours! Finally, the doctor asked Jasmin if his own, deceased mother was there. 'Yes,' came the reply. The Oxford don conveyed a cryptic message to his mother, one couched in terms which had special meaning for her only. Apparently, the answer indicated his mother had indeed received the message and understood it.

"The Chinese doctor was now convinced that something of a most interesting nature had been going on; but, as far as I know, no further investigation was ever made into the matter."

I wondered to myself: What did it all mean? Had Marie merely read the doctor's mind while she'd been in her trance? Or—?

Marie interrupted my thoughts to tell me once again that all guides are good and that they are working to further their own spiritual development. "There are many levels," she explained. "The spirits we contact are here"—she raised her hand to a place above her head—"then they ascend to a higher level as they advance spiritually, then higher, till the time of their ultimate union with God."

I asked her, "What exactly is the difference between a medium and a psychic?"

She answered, "When I work as a medium, I act only as a contact with the spirit world, in my case using Jasmin as my guide. I am merely a telephone. However, when I work as a psychic I use my own eyes and ears. We could bring so much good into the world if we would only heed our eyes and ears! Our insights, our intuitions, get buried. We need to refine them. That's why I'm giving up mediumship and spending all my time teaching those who have obvious powers of insight how to develop them.

"Besides, I'm getting older now," she continued, her fresh bright looks belying her words. "Trance work takes an enormous amount of energy and is quite physically draining. We mediums are highly sensitive people who work on wavelengths of emotion. In the trance state, my pulse rate accelerates to 140, stabilizing at 120. I have no reflexes whatsoever while in that state, and my pupils become widely dilated. Afterwards, I'm completely exhausted."

Marie commented that she found women made particularly good students. "Women have always had a certain inner knowledge, an inner awareness; they are closer to nature, closer to reality. Did you know that the word witchcraft was originally Wicca— the craft of the wise one, of the midwife, of the woman who instinctively knows which herbs can heal? When you teach women, it's almost as if you were reminding them of something."

I asked her why witchcraft had such a bad name. "I believe the prejudice arose," Marie replied, "because Wicca contained a ritual for concentrating the attention, a ritual that allowed women to gather their personal power. This led to Wicca's practice being feared as a religion through which females sought domination. Did you know that nine million witches were killed over a period of 150 years? I believe that psychic power is genetic, and that whole generations of psychics were lost to the world because of this. Those who would have passed on the gift genetically were killed. In this century, the gift is beginning to surface again." Marie's eyes brightened, "Yes, we are seeing it again to an appreciable degree. And this time it must be protected!"

Her voice grew tense: "If we could only advance spiritually as rapidly as we have materially. We're coming to the brink of disaster." She shook her head slowly. "But I have great hope." Her mood changed, as if she'd had a sudden insight: "I think...I think we will wake up before it is too late—."

As we parted, I asked her if she were able to use her clairvoyance for her own good.

"No. It's meant to be a totally unselfish gift. You don't find psychics making fortunes on the stock market, now do you, or winning at roulette? I can sense it when any member of my family is in danger, yes; but as for personal gain—never. No; it's an unselfish gift for the good of others."

My thoughts were racing as I left the sturdy old brick quarters of the College of Psychic Studies on Queensbury Street. It seemed to me that if the psychic gift did run in families, as Marie McDonald Cheerie had so strongly suggested, then, with modern technology, perhaps a genetic marker might one day be found, one which would serve to identify the gift early in a child's life.

And how intriguing this would be if it involved the seventh chromosome! Historically, many so-called "fortunetellers" have claimed to be "the seventh daughter of the seventh daughter."

Perhaps some inner awareness had caused them to choose the number seven.

Chapter 4

London, England: Introduction to a Distinguished Healer

I had heard from a number of sources about a remarkable British healer whom I was hoping to track down before I left London. Following the directions I'd been given, I made the long trip out to the remote London suburb of Muswell Hill. Here, guarded by a ginger-colored cat, in the sitting room of a tall Victorian house, I met the amazing Gwennie Scott.

Gwennie was a pleasant-looking woman with erect posture, short brown hair, and very gentle eyes. Nothing about her appearance suggested she was the custodian of astonishing secrets or possessed unusual powers. I said to myself that she looked to be in her mid-sixties. As if she'd read my mind—and also as if to explain her slow careful footsteps as we walked down the corridor leading from the door—she declared abruptly: "I'm in my eighties."

"How can you possibly look so young?" I exclaimed.

"Do I?" she countered. "I wouldn't know. I almost never look in the mirror. Mirrors can be so very aging. You must realize that when we look in the mirror we are thinking about ourselves, and self-preoccupation can add years to the face."

She led me through a high, wide doorway and indicated that I should take a seat on the long low sofa facing us. There must have been hundreds of rooms like this one scattered throughout the London suburbs: spacious and high ceilinged, with furnishings of a comfortably utilitarian bent. A scattering of personal mementos and a large black-and-white cat stretched lengthwise along the rug, gave to the room an additional infusion of character. I felt sure Gwennie wasn't particularly given to gazing around this well-lived-in room; probably, she evidenced toward it the same lack of personal vanity that made her avoid mirrors. Besides, you soon realized she didn't really live here at all; that her vision was entirely focused on another world.

"I move rather slowly these days," she said as she eased herself into a deep, overstuffed armchair. "I can't cure myself, can't seem to help myself at all." I wasn't surprised at her words. Other psychics have said as much, and I recalled the words of noted psychologist Eric Berne, who remarked that intuitive healing is more likely to be accurate when it involves others.

"How old were you when you first realized you had the gift of healing?" I asked her.

"At the ripe old age of four I was already known as a 'wart charmer,'" she said, laughing. "Sometimes, while walking to kindergarten, I would hold the hand of a little friend who had warts—inwardly with a sense of revulsion, I might add. I was always amazed to see the warts immediately disappear. I believe that was the beginning of my career as a healer. I've never lived in a fantasy world. I'm too practical for that. I've always wanted proof of everything in this life. Well, the warts disappeared. So, there it was!"

Would she tell me more about her childhood?

"Why not?" replied Gwennie in her wonderfully brusque manner. "Why not? It wasn't a very happy one. Oh, we had lots of things, things, things—physical comforts, a pretty house. But my parents were always preoccupied with their own activities, with little time to spare for their children. I remember feeling...well, not exactly neglected, but certainly not cherished. Do you understand?

"My name was Gwen Glover, and I suppose I was something of a prodigy. I was playing the piano with ease at the age of three. By the age of four or five, I was curing warts and lesions on my playmate's hand. But then, I've told you about that already, haven't I? Well, when I told my nurse and the chambermaids in the house that I cured warts, they only laughed and called me crazy. I soon stopped mentioning such things. By the time I was 13, I was a really accomplished pianist. Oh, yes; and, in the neighborhood, an accepted wart healer! My Victorian parents, who believed children should be seen and not heard, did little to encourage me in either of these pursuits."

There were frequent instances of premonitions. Gwennie learned to keep silent about them; there was no point in being ridiculed. Seeking some warmth and personal validation in her life, she married at the age of 18.

Unfortunately, this proved to be a most unhappy union. In her early twenties, Gwennie found herself alone again, this time with two small children to care for. Her life was becoming increasingly difficult. "No, you can't help yourself," she told me again. "The gift is always for others."

Gwennie now recalled an incident which, at that time in her life, underscored her unusual abilities as a clairvoyant. An itinerant salesman had come to the door, offering to sell her a lamp with a China shade. When she put out her hand to pay him, Gwennie lightly touched his hand. Immediately, she drew back. "But you're a murderer!" she whispered, forgetting the two little girls who were tugging at her skirts.

"Oh, you're one of *those*," the man exclaimed, his eyes widening in disbelief. "It's true. During the war, I killed a man in the desert for his boots. But you don't need to worry. I won't hurt you." The man turned away and slipped off quickly.

"Well, I should tell you this," Gwennie continued, "that even after I was grown up and on my own, there always seemed to be the necessary protection for me as well as the necessary food, the necessary clothing, the necessary shelter—but never anything more. And frankly, I'll tell you I wouldn't want more, for I might get caught up in the material world just as my parents were."

Having heard that many of Gwennie's clients were persons of great wealth, I presumed to point this out. "You could still be quite rich, you know, by treating the sick."

"Oh, I'd never, ever charge for a healing," she retorted, growing adamant. "It's a gift from the source of all life that directs my hand. I couldn't charge for that! And when I say I have healed someone, you realize I don't mean 'I.' I am only the instrument. The healing simply passes through my hands. The basis of all healing is love and compassion—and humility. The word 'humility' is so often misused. It has nothing to do with self-demeaning obsequiousness. Rather, it signifies a lack of ego, a recognition that God alone is the author of all that is good."

A turning point came in Gwennie's young life when she suffered a severe illness. Long, lingering months of acute pain brought into sharp focus her inherent sympathy for her fellow human beings. Accepting as a fact her innate gift for healing, she realized at the same time that she had little knowledge of anatomy. She knew that she would be better able to diagnose if she understood the functioning of the various parts of the body. With the help of her doctor, she assimilated information about human biology, and was soon treating a variety of illnesses.

"Don't forget," Gwennie told me, "it is up to each of us to use our own brains to keep ourselves healthy. We must learn to control our thoughts, but first we must be *aware* of our thoughts. One can lose control of the mind without going insane, you know. But loss of control can cause havoc in the body. Highly sensitive people must be doubly on guard. They seem to take in such a battery of stimuli from the outside. They should be very careful about the use of alcohol.

"I first realized the psychosomatic nature of many types of illness when I was quite young," she went on. "A woman came to me suffering from severe asthma. Without thinking, I immediately said to her, 'You don't have real asthma. Your husband recently died and your son was killed in the war. It is your deep sadness that is causing you your trouble.'"

I asked, "When someone comes to you for healing, what do you actually do?"

"Oh, they don't always have to come here, you know; I practice absent, or remote, healing as well, visualizing the illness to be treated and sending healing power. Space is no barrier to spiritual frequencies. Perhaps 'frequencies' isn't the right word; but there really isn't a proper word to express it. There are certain things that simply can't be described.

"When people come to me here, I place them on the sofa where you're seated and ask them to lie down. Then, I place my hand on the troubled area, and immediately they fall into a deep sleep. My hand—I usually use only one, for there is no increase in power with two, that simply divides the power between them—then I feel my hand being directed, and I often become totally unaware of myself as the spiritual power takes over. Sometimes, the healing is accomplished with one treatment; other times, it takes several."

I'm certain it was my look of total wonderment that caused her to add, quite humbly, "You see, my dear, I am attuned to the source of all life: God. I felt this even as a child. As I look back over my life, I realize that I had to live through my own little personal life dramas—two unhappy marriages, problems with the children, severe illnesses, loss of money and prestige—in order to learn to heal. Compassion had to be developed. I had to be able to get into a mental affinity with my patients.

"But don't misunderstand me. I don't think a psychic has any business telling someone's fortune! It could have too great an influence on that person. It could rule out free will."

Gwennie had discovered through the years that many people had a completely misdirected approach to life. "Our world is full of the unintentionally mendacious, people caught up in the confusion of daily living without knowing who they are or where they're going. The majority operate within the confines of their lower selves, where even their finest acts are inspired by motives not above suspicion. And, don't forget, so much is genetic," Gwennie concluded with a sigh.

"You do believe, though, that people can rise above their particular inherited characteristics?"

"Oh, yes. That was Christ's message! But don't go painting me as a saint," she cautioned. "I get upset over small frustrations just like anyone else."

I asked, "Do you think that Christ appeared on earth as a male because in the time and culture into which he was born, the sacrifice of a male would have been considered far greater than that of a female?"

"Oh, we could talk about that for hours," Gwennie said. And then she went on to speak, with sure knowledge and deep humility, about Christ and the disciples.

"Remember, my dear, we are all here for a purpose. Each of us has a purpose, whether we have a special gift or not. And fulfilling that purpose is one more step toward our ultimate goal, which is, of course, union with God." Her face grew pensive as she spoke about the future. "What do I see for the world? I am very, very discouraged. We are losing the spiritual essence of ourselves; we are forgetting who we are and how far we have evolved. We must not slip back!" Her eyes took on a look of sadness touched with nostalgia, as though she were remembering something that was both precious and important. "What is this life all about, with all its sufferings and frustrations, with all its seeming injustices? We will see, we will see—" Her thoughts seemed far away. Then she turned to me with a smile. Her voice became lighter:

"You asked me earlier about aging. Well, I believe our clock is set by the way we live. People imprisoned in a world of psychological fear age much faster than was intended for them. We must take our minds off ourselves. We must maintain a certain detachment from the material world. We must love our fellow man unconditionally, and never allow ourselves to feel resentment, if we want to remain young."

A well-known artist with multiple sclerosis would soon be arriving for treatment. It was almost time for me to leave.

"Before I go," I asked, "would you tell me about your most remarkable cure?"

"Oh, someday, my dear, someday, I may tell you. I don't think you would even believe it now."

The ginger-colored cat yawned and stretched its paws toward the small wall gas heater, while its black-and-white companion rearranged itself in a sluggish heap on the carpet. Gwennie Scott looked as rested and alert as when I'd first arrived. Leaving her tall Victorian house and walking rapidly toward the station, I hoped Gwennie would trust me enough one day to reveal the story of her finest healing. At this early stage in my search, I was still skeptical and questioning, and I probably wouldn't have believed her. Certainly, I could never have imagined then the impact that her revelation would one day have upon my life.

I changed trains at Victoria Station and headed back to Shipton-under-Wychwood. I had to pack for a flight to Italy the next day.

I couldn't stop thinking about Gwennie Scott and those rare souls like hers who must be scattered throughout the world. Their priorities, their aims, their thought processes—all follow a different path from ours. It's as though they're playing quite another game from the rest of us, one in which the goals are different and the rules entirely new. These people are beyond envy and the need to be envied. They are not interested in mankind's approbation or incentives. They have pitched their tents in another dimension, one where our rules don't apply.

Chapter 5

Rome, Italy: Signora De Filipo, Once Found, Holds Forth on Female Prophetic Power

Leaving the cool quiet of the English countryside and arriving in the oppressive heat of an August day in Rome prompts a person to wonder what effect climate might have on the visions of clairvoyance. Are the visions of the south different from those of the north?

On that day, the very buildings of Rome seemed as shimmering mirages, imparting to the entire city a strange and dream-like quality. Beneath the sweltering skies, tourists wandered like sleepwalkers among the ancient monuments, consulting their faded guidebooks through half-glazed eyes. We'd taken a flat near the Campodolio, one that in the late Renaissance had been part of a cardinal's palace; only its cool dark corridors afforded us any relief from the scorching heat.

I was wondering if a certain clairvoyant, known for her ability to predict the future with startling accuracy, might still be found here; or if, as was more likely the case, she had fled the city for a cooler climate. It would have taken no prophetic power to predict the pounding heat of a Roman August. Her name was Signora Anna De Filipo, and years had passed since I'd last seen her. She must be quite old now, I thought, perhaps even ill and sent off to die in one of those nursing homes run by nuns, or at the very best, housed in some other part of this steaming city. I'd once lived in Rome, and had known the city well; but I realized now with a start that I'd forgotten both her street number and her street.

Still, seeking out her old residence seemed to me the only way to begin the search. I knew the general area in Old Rome where she lived: on the right side of the Corso, just below the Piazza Navonna. So it was that I made my way to that wonderfully old and historic district; but, in its labyrinth of narrow streets, I soon found myself hopelessly lost.

There was, it suddenly occurred to me, someone who might be able to help me find Signora De Filipo. This was a rather elderly American spinster who had lived all her life in Rome, most recently, to the best of my knowledge, in two rooms in an old palace near the Bridge of Angels. That wasn't far from here.

The woman in question—Miss E.—had to be approaching 80 now. She was said to have had a series of glittering romances in her youth, all of them ending in disillusionment. When I knew her, the years were already beginning to hang heavy on her shoulders. Alone, still handsome, and with a small income from abroad, she had made her entire *raison d'être* come to center around embassy receptions. She left cards at each new ambassador's residence, sent greetings and congratulations on his National Day, Independence Day, Emperor's Birthday, Queen's Birthday—whatever was appropriate—in order not to be forgotten.

If an invitation to a reception failed to arrive, she was not above appearing uninvited, always careful to carry a clutch of old invitations in her purse—and to avoid the receiving line. In the unlikely event that her presence was questioned, she would quickly exhibit an invitation, glance at it in dismay, then exclaim, "Oh dear, I'm at the wrong party; I'm due at the *Grand*, or *The Excelsior*--", or she would name some obscure third-world embassy residence—and, head held high, gracefully disappear. The receptions became the focus of her entire week. She would change into her mended velvet dress, fasten on the slender strand of good pearls, sweep into a waiting cab—and still imagine herself a part of the city's *haute monde*.

I wondered if she were still alive and making the rounds, still leaving cards, still sending greetings. I hoped she was. Her embassy-hopping was a harmless enough pursuit, far better than growing bitter and contentious with the passing years. I remembered hearing that she often went to Signora De Filipo's for readings. So I made my way in the direction of Miss E.'s home; and, after a few wrong turns, I found the palace where, I thought, she most recently had lived.

But the porter's office was locked. The courtyard was deserted, its fern-encrusted fountain dry and silent in the scorching sun.

There was no way of knowing which of the many doorways led to the American's apartment. Two nuns passed by the front gate, their heavy woolen habits surely a penance in this grueling heat. There was no one anywhere to ask. I realized that my only hope lay in the retired American colonel through whom I'd first met Miss E. Whenever he and his wife had entertained, she'd always been somewhere in sight.

The colonel was a linear thinker who found it hard to cope with the Italian mentality and sought out his companions among the British and other English-speaking expatriates living out their lives in Rome. The fact that these fellow expatriates often had little in common seemed not to matter at all to any of them.

Telephoning from a nearby tobacco shop, I immediately obtained an invitation to tea from the colonel's Belgian wife. She grumbled to me that the two would be staying in town until after Ferragosto, the August holiday. "Can you imagine such a thing!" she fumed. "Rome in August! But we'll be leaving for the Dolomites in a week. You're lucky to have called us when you did."

I found the colonel looking much the same, though with less hair, perhaps, and with the addition of several pounds and a small neatly-trimmed moustache. The large glass case behind the entrance door still housed his prized collection of scrimshaw. After the usual embraces and exchanges of news, I began by saying, "I'm looking for an elderly American spinster whom I often met here at your parties. She lived in an old palace on the other side of Piazza—"

"You still use the term 'spinster?'" the Belgian wife interrupted loudly, fiercely arching an eyebrow. She had always been difficult; with her, a simple salutation could trigger off a confrontation. Once, I had even heard her greet a cheery, innocuous, "Good morning," with a challenging, "Are you wishing me a good morning? Or merely offering a subjective unsolicited opinion?"

Recalling this, I rallied for combat. "Why should using the term 'spinster' to describe an unmarried female be more pejorative than using the term 'bachelor' to designate a man who has never married?" I wanted to know.

The colonel carefully examined his shoelaces in order to avoid his wife's gaze. "Oh, yes, of course," he interjected, "you mean old Miss E.! She's in a nursing home near Tivoli now, I believe. She's no longer in her old flat."

Tivoli! Miss E. certainly wouldn't be making any visits to Signora De Filipo from there, I thought. "Actually, I'm looking for a clairvoyant that Miss E. told me she often visited, a Signora De Filipo," I said.

"That's easy," the Belgian wife snapped, "Signora De Filipo is on the Via dei Coronari, right around from Viccolo Savelli, not five minutes from here."

I drank my tea quickly lest there be further clashes, then said good-bye and hastened out in the direction of the Piazza. I crossed in front of a small *trattoria*, my nostrils suddenly catching the pungent aroma of fresh olive oil and garlic. I immediately thought of Irma Coombs Williams's pendulum, and I wondered if I would be able to take mine into a restaurant and, with everyone watching, somehow pass it surreptitiously over each succulent *entrée*.

Che figura! I thought. *What a spectacle that would make!*

Perhaps it would be best simply to take my chances and assume that all Italian foods, like all Italian people, were *simpatico*.

When at last I came to her address, I found Signora De Filipo still plump, still bustling, still very much alive, with her small neat apartment quite unchanged after all those years. The blinds were tightly shut against the heat outside; but, in the dimly-lit entrance hall, there was light enough to see that Signora De Filipo was quite unchanged except for two deep melancholy creases between her eyebrows.

For all her paranormal powers, there was nothing mystical about her appearance. It suggested the sort of hearty earthiness you associate with women who spend their lives close to the soil. She didn't seem at all surprised to see me after so many years: "Oh, I knew you were coming, Signora," she declared in answer to my question. "I always know when someone is coming. You want me to give you a reading, of course." All of this was spoken in rapid Italian with a musical lilt.

36

"No, no, I don't want a reading," I protested. "I only want the answers to some questions about you."

Directing me toward a chair, Signora De Filipo shrugged her shoulders and continued to shuffle a thick faded deck of cards.

"No, no," I repeated. "Leave the cards, please. I simply want to talk to you about yourself. I have a lot of questions to ask."

This wasn't going to be easy. My Italian, never brilliant, was going to be stretched to the limit.

"Don't worry, don't worry," said Signora De Filipo soothingly. "I understand that you're collecting information. Why are you collecting information? Oh, and you want to ask me some questions. Let's see what the cards say about this information that you're gathering."

"No, no, leave the cards out of this! Let's talk about you."

And so we began. I learned that her psychic ability had begun to manifest itself when she was five or six years old. She had had vivid dreams of events that would take place the following day or in the following weeks. She assumed that other people 'knew' what was going to happen, too. It came as a shock to her to learn otherwise; it left her feeling disturbed and isolated.

Signora De Filipo's adult life had been a happy if a simple one. Her greatest sadness was the recent death of her husband; its coming had caused her a long period of anxiety beforehand, since she had known intuitively just when he would die.

She told me her insights were heralded, or accompanied, by a strong sensation in the solar plexus. "I can feel when my friends are sick or in trouble, without being told. Yes, my younger daughter has inherited the ability, but she hasn't developed it yet. There now, that's enough about me. Let's run through the cards just once and see what they say about you."

"No, no, this is an interview," I insisted. "Tell me how you feel about your unusual gift."

"I try to use this gift, as you call it, to help others make sense of their lives. Intuition should be used to help, to protect, to advise."

I witnessed an example of Signora De Filipo's own particular intuition at work that same day, when I watched her talk to a shy

18-year-old who had dropped by for a reading. The Signora immediately sensed the girl was agoraphobic. "You become very anxious in open spaces," Signora De Filipo told her. "You experience feelings of panic, your heart races, and you have difficulty breathing." The girl nodded, her pale eyes widening. "How did you know?" she exclaimed. How indeed! An extremely observant person might have spotted, in the darting eyes and tight little mouth of this 18-year-old, something suggesting a neurosis; but, to pinpoint the nature of the problem so quickly—. "You must never, never take any alcohol," the Signora was warning the wide-eyed girl. "Not even a drop of wine! People who are nervous, who are precariously balanced, should never take strong drink. Your poor unhappy father was quite nervous; it is something which you have inherited, my dear."

The girl's cheeks turned crimson. "I don't want to talk about it," she muttered, looking anxiously down at her clenched palms.

Signora De Filipo's insights had hit the mark.

Moments later, I heard the Signora inform the next client, a handsome, smartly-dressed young woman from South Africa, that her husband had a serious heart condition he wasn't aware of. "It's very grave; he must be very careful," advised Signora De Filipo. "He should see a doctor at once." Despite the gravity of their content, her readings were always delivered in a soft, gentle voice with an undertone of cajolement.

When we were once more alone, the Signora began to philosophize. "As women grow stronger in influence, the world will improve," she pronounced. "But only if they bring their womanly instincts—their true feelings—into all their new endeavors. As women's influence grows stronger, this will force men to become better—or they will surely be diminished. No one wants men to be diminished, now do they?" Her eyes twinkled as she gave a hearty laugh.

We talked at length about the direction women's lives were taking. "Now, more than ever, women should develop their innate psychic abilities," Signora De Filipo proclaimed adamantly. "They must be their own guides. In the past, women have allowed themselves to be led. They must break that pattern, but not ex-change one set of shackles—is that the word?—for another. With her increased opportunities, a woman should try to find a path in harmony with her own highest instincts."

Then, for the first time since I had arrived, Signora De Filipo's face took on a worried expression; the two vertical creases between her eyebrows deepened. "I feel such sympathy for the women of this generation," she sighed. "They get so many confusing mes-sages from the world."

Yes, I thought, the old role models are *passé*, but the verdict isn't in on the new ones yet. It will be another generation or two before we'll be able to know if the direction women are now being led in—and "led" is still the operative verb—leads to a dead end street, or is the golden road to fulfillment.

We talked long into the afternoon. Signora De Filipo, for all her concern about the human condition, insisted that she still be-lieved we were all good "at the core." I looked at my watch sud-denly. "Oh, don't go," she exclaimed. Out came the cards again. "Please, let me give you a reading. We'll go through the cards just once." Once more, I demurred.

Signora De Filipo rose and walked me slowly toward the door.

"You know, my dear," she said in parting, "the great threat to the world today is drugs. But the problem is with people them-selves. If they could only go within and find their essential good-ness, they would not need drugs!"

I said good-bye; she kissed me warmly on both cheeks. As I was racing down the stairs and out into the noisy street below, she called after me in a voice that had regained its customary lilt: "Next time, Signora! Next time, we'll run through the cards, won't we?!"

On the way back to the hotel, I recalled her words: "We're all good at the core." I thought of *The Gnostic Gospels*, that contro-versial document found some 50 years ago at Nag-Hammadi, with its frequent admonitions to us to seek the good within ourselves. Perhaps man's original mistake lay simply in his failure to realize that he was created in the image and likeness of God—his failure to understand that, "It is your Father's good pleasure to give you the

Kingdom." Wasn't that the essence of Christ's message? Doesn't most aberrant behavior stem from low self-esteem?

Perhaps this was where the Church had failed. By concentrating on man's sins, it had forfeited sufficient emphasis on man's birthright in the "image and likeness." The Gnostics believed the cause of all suffering, sin, and sickness was bound up with the material universe, of which our physical bodies were certainly a part. Only by an "interior journey" into one's own spirit could peace and joy be found, for the essential self, contended the Gnostics, is divine—"The Kingdom of God is within you."

Internationally known consciousness researcher Dr. Charles Tart has concluded that our true natures are "vast and glorious and God-like, and beyond our ordinary conceptions." Whatever we may believe, it might be well to ask whether the "sixth sense" is one of a series of doors leading inward to the ultimate good within ourselves. We might reflect that, if goodness is the source of all knowledge, then evil must simply be ignorance. We might even conclude, with psychologist/author Jean Houston, that aberrant acts are simply "unskilled behavior."

Chapter 6

Ostia, Italy: The Psychic Who
Dreamed Her Death and Saved Her Life

The following day, I took a train out to the Lido di Ostia, some 25 miles south of Rome on the West coast. It was a Sunday, and I was hoping to meet Nancy Circelli Wodehouse, a talented painter who had a reputation for making accurate psychic predictions. Nancy was living with her British husband on the Via Ammiraglio Marzola, in Ostia, at the time, in a penthouse overflowing with lush green plants. I'd heard she'd given up her studio in Rome.

Nancy was a tall brunette whose warm smile and dark penetrating eyes made me feel immediately welcome. Her husky voice had an attractive urgency which lent to her every statement the weight of a pronouncement. I asked her about her childhood.

"My childhood?" Nancy began. "My childhood was terrible!"

Her eyes stared absently off into the distance as she spoke. She had been the eldest of five children born into an affluent Italian-American household. Her father had lost everything in the stock market crash of 1929 and had deserted the family. The subsequent years were ones of despair born of homelessness, hunger, and the tragic death of her only brother. As a result of those trying years, Nancy's mother's became mentally unbalanced. The poor woman hadn't been able to accept or even to grieve for her son's death. Still in her teens, Nancy had the sole responsibility for the entire family. She was also the object of frequent violent attacks on the part of her mother. The relatives refused to help, rejecting any suggestion of mental illness.

Nancy had a vivid prophetic dream one night. She dreamed that her mother had locked all the doors in Nancy's bedroom except for one hidden behind a very high bed—a door Nancy had never known existed. Nancy then dreamed that her mother began attacking her. Several days later, the mother actually did enter

41

Nancy's room, lock the door, and launch a vicious, knife-wielding assault upon her daughter. Terrified, Nancy tried to protect herself; bleeding, with her clothes torn, she suddenly remembered the door behind the bed in the dream. Somehow, Nancy managed to push the heavy bed aside and pin her mother to the wall—and there indeed was an unlocked door through which Nancy could escape. The dream had saved her life.

Subsequently, Nancy was forced to commit her mother to a mental institution. This was the time of the Great Depression. Nancy's life became a frantic struggle for survival as, desolate and alone, she tried to care for herself and her younger sisters.

While Nancy was telling her story, I was struck by her appearance of serene detachment; it was as if those years had left no scars upon her. Perhaps, I thought, she had arrived at that enlightened state where you realize the unimportance of your own personal history and understand that spiritual growth is all that matters.

The difficult period continued in the life of the youthful Nancy, and she became seriously ill. Lying in bed with a burning fever, she dreamt that she felt her dead grandmother's cool hands touching her forehead. She awakened completely well.

As she grew older, Nancy moved to another part of the country. It was there that she began increasingly to have psychic insights. The illuminations were always preceded by a strange sensation and a desire to sleep. Nancy was unhappy in her new home, and she would often escape into the forest to meditate and be alone. Her illuminations became stronger. Whenever there was a disaster, such as a plane crash, with pictures of passengers shown in the news reports, Nancy would 'know' which ones had been killed and which ones injured, even before the authorities had made the determination. She recalled a particularly vivid prophetic dream. She 'saw' a plane clearing the tops of oil derricks, then crashing into a row of houses. She 'saw' people running from the wreckage in flames. Badly shaken, she woke up and telephoned a friend to describe the dream to him. Later, the friend called back, telling her to, "Turn on the TV!" Nancy did so, and learned that the accident, just as she had seen it in her dream, had actually occurred many miles away, on a Raymond Street in Signal Hill. She, Nancy, was living on a Raymond Street in Glendale!

Nancy warned me that a person had to be very strong in order to handle the power of psychic dreams and insights. "You mustn't go after them; you must let them come to you," she flatly stated. "If you're continually seeking them like some mediums do you'll end up straddling two worlds, and eventually the other will take possession of you. Then you'll be unable to cope. The power is awesome," she insisted, "and should be used for good." With this power, Nancy had been able to save lives by sensing a sickness developing in someone long before it had physically manifested. She felt her own acute suffering as a child had left her with great sympathy and compassion for others, and an ability to 'sense' each person's particular pain.

Nancy had a strong Christian faith. She was convinced God would always send the answer so long as she "kept the channel clear." She asserted that, "Psychics should never exploit their gifts for money, unless this is absolutely necessary in order for them to live. The psychic gift is a gift for helping others."

Nancy described how she sometimes dreamed "futuristically"— an ability that led her to believe that time was merely a concept. "We travel back and forth in time," she explained, "hence déjà vu." Nancy could not understand why so little attention was being paid to psychics. "Lincoln and other leaders have used 'sensitives,' that is, persons capable of extrasensory perception; clairvoyance is an awesome power, deserving of more respect."

Nancy's first marriage had been to a Russian émigré named Kuminsky. Unfortunately, he had suffered a childhood as miserable as her own; but, instead of spiritual growth, his early years had led him to a gradual deterioration into schizophrenia. Nancy felt, as many do, that schizophrenia has a chemical basis; she was convinced that, in her husband's case, that illness had been triggered by immense stress. Nancy spoke to me quite dispassionately about this trial in her life. The marriage ended in divorce and, alone once more, Nancy took comfort in her painting which was then beginning to receive acclaim.

The fates, however, were not yet finished with her. A son born to this marriage developed cystic fibrosis, and the doctors were certain he would die. It was only due to Nancy's intuition and constant care through the long years of his illness that the boy had survived and flourished. I got the distinct impression, as she told her story, that the boy's recovery had marked a happy turning point in Nancy's own struggle to survive. Even so, through all her trials she had never once succumbed to bitterness. She was always aware of this power of insight within her—a power that held so much promise.

"Sometimes," she told me, "in a simple mundane setting like a motel lobby, the scene will suddenly be flooded with light and an unbearable sense of beauty! I feel in those moments as if I have glimpsed 'reality,' and a great sense of peace fills my mind."

Her eyes grew distant. "Humanity has survived terrible times, and we will survive the days ahead. The good we think and do creates an energy that will appear in others. We are all connected.

"Sensitives should be most careful," Nancy cautioned me. "Their best protection is to stay close to God. I believe that sensitives, in drawing on their intuition and insight, can help the world find a way out of its problems. But that way must come from within each individual. What we want from a foreign government—or from our own government—we must demand of ourselves. Whatever you seek in another, or in a collective other, you must first seek in yourself."

Nancy leaned forward in her chair to stress the point she was about to make. "Thoughts are things. Until we guard their purity with the same caution with which we guard our water supply, or our food from contamination, we are in danger of sickening ourselves and others." She was silent for a moment. "We sensitive women certainly do become philosophers, don't we?" she finished up. Her eyes twinkled and she gave a hearty laugh.

I asked her: "If we are searching for a higher reality, how should we go about it?"

"Try doing a good deed," Nancy told me with a smile. "In any good deed or any genuine thought or act of unselfishness, there is a release of energy as it goes into another, and it will give the sender a fleeting feeling of warmth. It's a first step for the unenlightened."

It was growing dark outside, and I had a long trip back to Rome to make. I said goodbye to Nancy and her husband. As I boarded my train, I noticed an advertisement on the station wall for a local insurance company. I wondered if after all such companies weren't a force for good in the world, not merely because they saved people from bankruptcy in the event of disaster, but because every day they bet their livelihood that nothing calamitous is going to happen. It seemed to me that therefore they must consciously or unconsciously put positive thoughts into the atmosphere.

Nancy had spoken with great urgency about guarding our thoughts. Was this how, despite all the odds, she had been able to turn her luck around? Philosopher-mystic P. D. Ouspensky reminds us in his writings that any given lifetime is the fulfillment of but one of myriad possibilities. "As a man thinketh in his heart...," was not simply meant in a judgmental sense, but to assure us that we have a large measure of control over which of these myriad possibilities would be fulfilled. Our random, uncensored thoughts influence our destiny just as much as do our conscious choices. As Charles Darwin said, "The highest possible stage in moral culture is when we recognize that we ought to control our thoughts."

We are, after all, the sole curators and conservators of our memories—which are the sum total of our thoughts—so it is we, ourselves, who "imagine" the history of our lives.

Nancy Cirelli Wodehouse had given me a great deal to think about. I wanted to hear more, especially concerning her ideas about the nature of time. But perhaps we would meet again. Perhaps, in the timeless past, we had already met.

In the months to come, I would remember Nancy's emphasis on the power of thought. I would reflect on her description of the release of energy which always follows a genuinely unselfish act. There would come a time when I would vividly recall her words; and I would wonder if they just might not explain the mysterious recovery by Caroline Henry of the sight of one eye—a baffling healing about which we will learn in a later chapter.

Chapter 7

Titular Spirit of Capri

The next time I boarded the Rapido, it was to head for Naples. I was eager to pay a visit to the island of Capri. It would be cooler there than in Rome, and there was a chance I might be able to locate the much-renowned medium Signora Buronzo, reported to be living on Capri—or was it Anacapri? No one I talked to knew for sure.

Arriving on the island late in the day, I waited till morning to look for Signora Buronzo. The search wasn't easy; each unsuccessful lead led to another, until I was told that if anyone knew her whereabouts it would be Manfredi Pegano, a 94-year-old gentleman who had been born on Capri and was reputed to have an encyclopedic knowledge of its inhabitants. Finding Signore Pegano proved no small feat in itself; information about him was contradictory, and the directions I was given were vague and confusing.

Heeding a shop owner who spoke with a degree of certainty, I was soon winding my way down an endless labyrinth of sunlit alleyways bounded on either side by high stone walls ablaze with bougainvillea. I came at last to a narrow entrance at the back of a worn stucco building. I had been told that "one flight up at the end of a long corridor," Signor Pegano had his apartments.

The foyer was a jumble of paintings, sofas, and cabinets filled with curios. It led into a large drawing room filled with more paintings, sofas and cabinets, and more curios and more memorabilia. Fine porcelain crockery nestled cheek to jowl with brightly-colored rocks and gleaming African woodcarvings. A small stuffed alligator leered menacingly at a bronze head of Aphrodite—and everywhere were scattered books, pamphlets and endless stacks of papers. It would take months to inventory all of this material, which seemed to be what Signor Pegano was just then in the process of doing.

My gaze returned to the venerable gentleman himself, who had opened the door for me and was now giving me a little bow of greeting. Signor Pegano was small and lean, with sun-parched, wizened features and sunken eyes that still gave off a lively sparkle. His smile immediately conveyed a wealth of kindness. "Who has sent you?" he asked earnestly. "How can I help you? No, I speak no English. But come, your Italian is fine."

"Where can I locate the Signora Buronzo?" I asked.

"Signora Buronzo, Signora Buronzo—but she's dead now, isn't she?" He peered around the room as if looking for confirmation. "Oh, she was quite wonderful," he exclaimed with a happy smile, "a real medium who worked with tapping tables. Come, come over here." He pointed through the open window. "That is the house where she used to live."

A sun-washed white stucco villa, bright with azaleas, seemed an unlikely spot for shadowy seances. But Signor Pegano knew everything, and so I knew he must be right.

"Too bad you missed her," he pronounced wistfully. "There has been no one like her here since. She died only a year ago. It's too bad you missed her.

"Here," he gestured toward the couch, "let me move these papers so you can sit down—over here, near the window. My eyes aren't so good anymore. What can I tell you? My father knew her well!"

Before I could say anything, he went on: "My grandfather had the first hotel in Capri. In 1820, it opened. English and Americans mostly at first—then artists, singers and writers from all over began to come. Look at this!" Shuffling across the room, he picked up an oddly shaped parcel; unwrapping it, he drew forth a glazed terracotta dish displaying a bas-relief portrait of opera singer Enrico Caruso. "Caruso did this himself," he declared proudly. "Did you know that he was a sculptor as well as a singer? He gave it to my grandfather. And—look at this!"

Signor Pegano advanced toward me holding an ancient hotel registry bound in worn leather. He slipped something from between the pages. "Here is a letter from Hans Christian Andersen to my father, praising the hotel." He offered for my inspection some faded signatures that were in the volume. "Everyone came—

everyone!" He repeated these words over and over, eyes now focused far away.

Signor Pegano slowly replaced the book on the ancient sagging sofa, along whose length were stacked a century-and-a-half of jumbled papers and records awaiting their final resting place in the Capri historical museum.

He suddenly recalled my presence. Looking impishly at me, he declared, his ancient eyes glittering: "Well, dear lady, I wish I could help you find Signora Buronzo. But I don't suppose either one of us want to be seeing her just yet, now do we?"

I left the old gentleman in his cluttered maze of memories and wound my way back up through the labyrinth of alleys. Soon, I was on the Rapido and headed back for Rome. If I hadn't been able to find the lady who could summon spirits, I had at least found someone who was able to summon a wealth of memories—who, indeed, could almost have been the titular spirit of Capri itself.

Chapter 8

Rome, Italy: Hovering Spirits
in the Parioli District

If Ruth Baher had been hidden away in some remote Asiatic village, speaking only in enigmatic aphorisms and accessible only to a few intrepid pilgrims, she might be revered today as a sort of latter-day sibyl. Perhaps by now she would even have acquired her own coterie of disciples.

The truth was that dynamic, British-born Ruth Baher worked by day as a dental hygienist and in the evenings happily welcomed friends and acquaintances to her brightly furnished flat in the upscale Parioli district of Rome. Here, her "breezy" down-to-earth manner seemed oddly incongruous in the light of the astonishing psychic readings that she gave.

Night after night, nonchalantly swinging a small metal pendulum above a square of paper packed with words, she off-handedly proceeded to apprise her friends of facts about their lives which only they could know. With an unconcerned toss of her head she seemed to delight in divulging the unexpected and leaving her clients in a state of undisguised shock. During the first sitting, clients were bombarded with inconsequential trivia: what they'd had for breakfast, the arthritic shoulder that was giving them trouble, the nationality of a new business associate, where a missing button could be found—all of this, accurate information, deadly accurate! I supposed this was how Ruth Baher established her credentials. On subsequent visits, she dealt with the more important aspects of the subject's life; there were messages from departed friends, advice, predictions—and enough personal information to confound the most hardened skeptic. Such was the sequence when I underwent my own readings. Thoroughly shaken when they had concluded, I asked Ruth, "How are you getting all this?"

"It's easy!" came her good-natured if abrupt reply. "There are spirits all around us, here in this room, everywhere. I'm in touch with them. *They* move the pendulum; *they* give me the answers."

49

I pressed her for more. "How long has this been going on?"

"For me, it started when I lost my sister. For a long time, I was very sad—in a deep depression, really. Then, one day, she got in touch with me. I knew she was near me. I can't explain it, but I soon realized there were spirits all around us. The spirits give all the answers."

I was still unable to accept this idea of hovering spirits. I ventured to suggest, "Couldn't some part of your brain simply be picking up information from the client's subconscious?"

Ruth laughed heartily. "No, absolutely not! This has nothing whatsoever to do with my brain. We're talking about another dimension entirely!"

I was unconvinced, but, certainly, I had no basis on which to argue. So the discussion ended.

"Oh, my dear," she exclaimed, jumping to her feet, "I haven't offered you anything to drink!"

"No, thank you, and I really must go," I murmured. I'd managed to reply in a fairly normal voice, but I was still thoroughly dazed by all I'd seen and heard.

Mulling it over afterward, I was a little confused—and also a little angry. I thought: How dare we take people like Ruth Baher lightly? Here were people like her, living among us unnoticed and unheralded, going quietly about their daily chores—shopping for supper, ironing the clothes, feeding the cats—and unaware, perhaps themselves as much as we, of the awesome significance of what they were able to do. How could the scientists—all of them evolutionists of one stripe or another—failed to have asked the question, "What exactly is happening here?"

For that question gave birth to others: Was a new species emerging, one not solely dependent on the five senses for information? Had mankind been, from his earliest appearance on the earth, programmed for a higher awareness than that which he now demonstrated? If the answer to either of these was yes, how could we set about to activate this potential? And this takes us back to the subject of those who are already, in varying degrees, demonstrating these powers: Should we not be diligently studying, with every resource we have at hand, the astonishing anomalous behavior demonstrated by some human beings?

Almost without realizing it, I had gone from being a skeptic to being a believer. Now I was on my way to becoming a crusader.

Chapter 9

Florence, Italy:
Psychic Healer of the Animal World

My meeting with Ruth Baher had left me quite shaken. I thought it would be best to retreat to the familiar for a day or two, before seeking out any further encounters with the spirit world.

On the strength of this decision I telephoned two long cherished friends in Florence whose feet were planted firmly in the here and now. Putting aside all otherworldly concerns, I set out early next morning on the three-hour drive which would take me to their flat near the banks of the Arno River.

I found my friends as warm and delightful as ever. We laughed over the recent political elections; they brought me up-to-date on the latest exhibitions; we exchanged amusing scraps of news about our mutual friends. I was on terra firma again, back in the real world. My stay promised to be a pleasant hiatus from my heady explorations of the occult.

The doorbell rang, and the small, white-gloved maid put down the tray she was carrying and slipped quietly out of the room to answer the door. My hostess rose immediately. "I've invited an English friend, June Adams, to join us for lunch," she told me. Then she added, "Well, actually, June was born in Florence, though her father was English and her mother was American." My friend pointed out the window, across the swiftly flowing Arno. "She's spent most of her life here, over there, right across the river, so we really consider her a Florentine."

She took my arm and, motioning to her husband to follow, led me out onto the sun-filled *loggia*. She lowered her voice to a conspiratorial whisper: "There's something very interesting about June I should tell you. She has an amazing affinity with animals, sort of an odd intuition where they're concerned. You can ask her about it; she won't mind."

Oh, no, I thought, here we go again! It's no longer a question of how can I find a female psychic; it's a question of how can I avoid them!

Just at that instant, June Adams, who had been let in by the maid, stepped out onto the *loggia*. And, at that exact moment, the two cats who were sleeping in a far corner suddenly got up, stretched, and padded over to her side. As June sat down, they leapt onto her lap and immediately fell asleep.

These two felines were a recent addition to the household; they had seen neither me nor June before.

June Adams was tall, almost stately in bearing, with a gentle manner and a soft, low-pitched voice. She told me her rapport with animals went back to her childhood, when people had thought of her as something of a pied piper of the animal world. Like all sensitives who feel an empathy toward animals, June was guided by intuition in her handling of them. Apparently, the animals sensed what she called her 'basic instinctual understanding'—and responded. Though June was shy and reticent to speak about her gifts, she admitted to having healing hands—certainly, where animals were concerned—and, through her healing touch, had restored many an ailing or injured beast to health.

I asked if she had any intuitive insights not involving animals.

"Well, yes," June Adams replied almost reluctantly, after a long pause. "But these insights occur quite at random, you know. I can never tell when they're going to come. But there have been some interesting consequences on occasion. One stands out particularly in my mind. During the Second World War, the son of an old friend of mine was shot down over Sicily. 'Over Sicily' was all we knew. No one had any additional clues as to his whereabouts.

"I suddenly quite vividly 'saw' him. I was able to pinpoint the precise spot where his body lay. I can't explain how I did this. I really don't understand it at all."

June sat quietly for a moment. Then she admitted almost shyly to having a gift for dowsing. "I've quite often been able to sense the exact location of water," she told me. "But," she was quick to add, "I haven't done that for a long time."

53

The small, white-gloved maid announced that lunch was served, and the conversation turned to more mundane topics. I later learned from my hosts that, though she spent the greater part of her time among the artists and *literati* of Florence, June Adams's abiding interest lay not surprisingly in supporting the various organizations throughout the world that worked for animal protection.

June said good-bye to us shortly after coffee, pleading a 3:00 p.m. appointment with members of an animal welfare group.

When she rose to leave, the two sleeping cats awoke, got up, slowly stretched, and followed her quietly to the door.

Chapter 10

Provence, France: A Psychometrist Sees a Shipwreck 300 Years Ago

A neighbor of mine has a decided weakness for antiques. Those not inherited from a conglomerate of widely scattered relatives, she has picked up from heaven knows where in the course of her travels. These antiques retain, she has always insisted to me, a bit of the essence of their former owner, just as an old fur piece retains faint traces of its owner's perfume. "It's *there*," my neighbor breathes, "in the wood, in the marble—*something*."

She loves to speak in particular about the "invisible footprints" on the threadbare Aubusson rugs that carpet her floor. "Have you ever sat in silence in an empty opera house?" she once asked me, "or sat blindfolded in one of the great museums? Thoughts, sounds, colors, designs—they all give off their own unique energy. You can feel that energy continuing to vibrate."

The comments of my friend made me think of Arthur Koestler's observation that the stones of a prison are not the same as the stones of a cathedral, even though they may come from the same quarry.

This conversation came vividly to mind while I was making my way southward from Paris toward the Mediterranean region of Provence. An old friend of mine, owner of a piece of property in the peaceful region just above Arles, had promised to locate the psychic Katherine Lopez for me. Katherine, said to be living in the area, was known to possess the gift of psychometry—the power to acquire information about an object merely by touching it.

My friend did manage to locate Katherine, and the three of us met at her house. Katherine, I learned, had been born the daughter of Polish emigrants who had settled in the north of France. She described her childhood to me as a most unhappy one. Her softly accented voice descended to a whisper as she painfully recalled her early years: the death of her beloved mother and her own deep sense of sorrow and abandonment.

At the age of seven, Katherine had begun to have premonitions, to 'see' visions and 'hear' voices. She had quickly repressed these 'knowings,' believing them to be at odds with her Catholic upbringing. Later, when she found that none of her classmates experienced similar insights, her sense of loneliness and isolation only increased.

It wasn't until her early twenties that Katherine began to accept and appreciate her unusual gifts. The turning point came unexpectedly. One day while she was saying her rosary and concentrating on the words, she found herself filled with a burning sensation and felt "ablaze inside with a blue light." She somehow felt "at one with the present, and that the present was all there was." She felt she was "in communication with all the earth, and all of nature, and moving further out, with the entire universe." She described this experience as a "pulsating feeling of oneness," which lasted only a brief moment but changed her life forever.

In our converation she switched the topic abruptly to her everyday routine. Katherine told me she had many friends and a rich cultural life centered around her work in the theatre; she felt people were in no way intimidated by her powers. She particularly enjoyed her healing work; in this work, she was often able to diagnose an illness long before it fully manifested in the body. She did not fraternize with other psychics, as so many of them 'invoked the spirits,' a practice of which Katherine disapproved. She didn't deny the existence of 'spirits' or 'energies;' but she felt such entities were still ego-bound, and therefore couldn't be of much help.

I asked Katherine if she felt that she had a particular mission. She replied, "No, because thinking of it in that way would be putting emphasis on my own ego."

Katherine believed that negative emotion would diminish a psychic's power, because such emotions produced bad energy and caused blocks. She hoped she was beyond such feelings now. Though she was sure she had no spirit guide as such, she had often felt the presence of energies directed toward helping her. "You can't put a name on energy," she told me, "because there is no ego involved that would give itself a name. There are many energies between God and earth, and a medium must use them to help others become clean. There is one God, and mediums must ask God's help to remain pure in order that they may use their energies to help others become pure. The gift would surely diminish if it were used to cause harm; a medium must be pure at all times." Katherine expressed all this with the greatest feeling.

"Are all mediums so dedicated to doing good?" I asked.

She shook her head. "You see," she explained, "psychic ability can be developed by many; it is my belief that a residual part of the primitive brain still retains this ability. But it must be purified, or it will only work cunning."

I recalled that Patricia Treece, in her well-researched book *The Sanctified Body*, had emphasized that the psychic gift was spiritually neutral *per se*—just as, I supposed, you could say that intellectual gifts were spiritually neutral, and might be used for either good or ill.

Katherine felt that the ever-creating energy of God demanded only one thing, that we love one another. "And a mystic, one who sees behind and in front, has the greater responsibility not to be prideful." Because of their education and place in society, women possessed these mystic qualities more than men; lacking physical and economic powers, they had had to become more sensitive in order to survive. Still, she warned, "in this changing world, women should always remain women. They should be equal but different. Men and women are meant to complement each other."

Katherine prayed that God would help all psychics to constantly purify themselves. "These are changing times," she stated. "Sensitives who have the ability to see the world in great clarity can be of so much help." She felt there must be a change of mindset if humanity wished to survive.

I wasn't surprised to hear once again that psychics must keep themselves pure; it's generally agreed that the psychic gift is an unstable one, and can vary from day to day.

Katherine, like many other psychics, told me that when she experienced an illumination, she felt a strong sensation in the area of the solar plexus. She told me she believed that people create their own destiny, and added that she was able to pick up vibrations and predict the future a client would attract into his or her environment. She insisted that she only concentrated on these vibrations when asked. "To be probing uninvited would be like a medical doctor at a dinner party taking someone's pulse unasked," she explained. "No, in all social intercourse, I simply enjoy and accept whatever mask is presented to me."

When she gave a reading she often used the Tarot cards, but only to provide a focus when the illuminations began to come.

Katherine would not read for everyone. Sometimes, she sensed a coldness around her when she received a request, and felt that the motives behind it were wrong. She refused such requests; she would only work when she felt she could help someone for his or her good or spiritual growth.

As a result of a shattering experience of her own, Katherine was a firm believer in reincarnation. Although she was a Polish Catholic, who had been born into this life in the 1950s, she felt certain that she had been Jewish in her last reincarnation and a victim of the Holocaust. She told me that when she was still quite young she had been taken to Jerusalem where, suddenly—with no previous knowledge of the language—she had found herself able to understand the Hebrew being spoken around her. She had even begun to join with complete ease in the conversations. Added to this feeling of certainty that she'd once been Jewish was the fact that on her single trip to Germany she had experienced without apparent cause a feeling of such uneasiness and sadness that she had immediately packed her bags and left.

Now we digressed to the subject of language itself. The circumstances in which and through whom a person learns a language can be a defining influence, we decided, since words are always emotionally loaded. If a child has had a disadvantaged or traumatic childhood, a change to an environment requiring a whole new language may perhaps help to mitigate future suffering.

I asked her finally to tell me more about her renowned gift for "psychometry"—the ability to hold an object and sense what had gone on in and around it. She answered by describing a recent experiment in which her powers had been tested. Katherine had been handed a small fragment of a china dish recovered from the wreckage of a ship. "The ship had sunk off the coast of Gabon nearly 300 years ago," she explained. Through the power of psychometry, she had 'known' how the ship had gone down; she had 'felt' the diseased condition of the seamen and immediately 'heard' the bullets as a near mutiny took place. When the historical documents were examined, they proved her account in the main to be correct. "There was no way of checking some details," she told me, "and others are still being studied."

Katherine greatly enjoyed her present life, but she had never forgotten the glimpse of reality she received so many years ago. "I'm always working to attain that state," she told me happily, "because I know that such a state exists."

Chapter 11

Medjugorje, Yugoslavia: Joy of the Children Who See the Virgin Mary

The ecstasies described in the vast literature devoted to the lives of the saints appear never to be accompanied by sharp sensations in the solar plexus, or strange sensations in the head. In their moments of "illumination," the saints, even though mortally ill or starving or undergoing physical torture, speak only of a transcendent joy. These facts had caused me to wonder if the clairvoyance that is often said to appear as a by-product of sanctity was the same as the "spiritually neutral" clairvoyance that we have been talking about.

It seemed to me that physical sensations might provide a clue. I was eager to learn how the experience of the mystic might differ in its physical manifestations from the experience of the psychic. That was why, shortly before the outbreak of war in Yugoslavia, I journeyed to the village of Medjugorje, in the mountains of Bosnia-Herzegovinia; it was here that, beginning in June, 1981, six children claimed to be able to see and talk to the Virgin Mary.

These children insisted that, with only a few exceptions, the Virgin appeared to them every evening at 6:00 p.m., with messages that she hoped they would transmit to the world. In addition to these messages, there were often personal admonitions for each child. The children had been interviewed by psychiatrists, by the clergy, and by news media from all over the world. They had been continuously submitted to every possible test in an effort to 'break their story.' Through all this, the children had remained calm, courteous, and poised; and, according to those who had known them since birth, they had become quite visibly "more refined."

The appearance of the village of Medjugorje itself gradually changed in the years that followed the first reports of the vision. Almost from the start, busloads of pilgrims began to arrive daily. To accommodate the hordes of visitors, farmhouses had to be enlarged and inside plumbing installed. Small restaurants sprang up along the narrow roads, and souvenir stands from the outside world mushroomed almost overnight.

Despite this sudden loss of anonymity, the village people themselves were said to have changed for the better. There was no more quarreling, and no undue eagerness to exploit a potentially profitable situation. A sense of peace prevailed as prayer and fasting were practiced by the families of the parish.

Mary was reported to have said, "Christians have forgotten that they can stop wars and even natural calamities by prayer and fasting." She had pointed out that the Catholics, especially those who live in villages like Medjugorje, separate themselves too much from the Serbs and from persons of the Muslim faith. She had always affirmed that there was only one God and that people had divided themselves, once reminding the children, "You are not a Christian if you do not respect others, Muslims and Serbians as well." Many outstanding healings had taken place spontaneously since Mary had first appeared, but she had said she was not responsible for these healings, that they came from God.

Each day there was a message, and sometimes also a personal message for one of the visionaries in particular. More often, the messages were general, and intended for the entire world; these usually consisted of urgent pleas for conversion and peace, for prayer and fasting, for the love of one's neighbor. "Don't think about wars, chastisements, evils," was a recurrent refrain. "It is when you are concentrating on these things that you are on the way to entering into them."

There were also the "ten secrets" which were gradually being revealed to all the children. At the time of my visit to Medjugorje, one of the visionaries, Miranga, had received all ten, which was why the Virgin no longer appeared to her except on her birthday. I was told that another child had already received nine; and another, seven or eight. It was said that, when all the secrets had been given to all six of the children, then, on a specific date not yet revealed to them, they might reveal the secrets to the world. People were to prepare themselves spiritually for this moment, for it was believed the secrets had to do with mitigating an impending world catastrophe. The children had resisted every possible form of persuasion exercised to entice them to reveal the secrets. Marija had even been questioned under hypnosis—to no avail.

When I was at Medjugorje, there was an exact procedure that the children followed every evening and that I was able to observe. At about 5:35 p.m., the six quietly entered the second floor of a small building located on the church grounds; they were followed by newsmen, priests, nuns, and as many of the infirm and their bearers as could be squeezed into this limited space. On a table were small objects that had been placed there to be blessed; facing that table, the children began to pray the "Our Father," the "Hail Mary," and the "Glory Be."

Suddenly, the young visionaries gave forth exclamations and fell to their knees in concert, their eyes fixed on a spot above their heads. Their lips continued to move, but their voices were silent. They seemed to be conversing with what they were seeing. After 15 or 20 minutes, their normal expressions returned, and they rose to their feet and silently filed out. As they left, the crowds pressed all around them, trying to touch them.

It's important to note that, on any particular evening, each child always disclosed the same message, and their descriptions of what they 'saw' were always identical.

On an unusually hot afternoon, I set out with my interpreter up a hilly road leading out of the center of town. I was in search of Marija Pavlovic, eldest of the six children. Her house wasn't hard to identify, since its small yard and the stone steps leading up to her door were packed with Italian pilgrims straining to catch a glimpse of the youthful visionary. It was only after these pilgrims had left to make their way down the dusty hill to the church that I was able to speak with Marija.

She bore herself with great dignity and poise. Her eyes were calm and level. With the help of the interpreter, I was able to put my questions to her about the physical sensations which accompanied her experiences. Marija replied quietly that, when the visions manifested themselves, she had no particular physical sensations at all—simply an overwhelming sense of joy which left her with a feeling of indescribable peace.

What was the worth and truth of what I heard? We have difficulty understanding those who have glimpsed a reality we have not. But if reality is, as it is so often described, a "consideration agreed upon," then we have to remember that these six children were in complete agreement as to what they saw and heard. The opinion of the Church, or the skepticism of the lay world, was of little importance to them. For them, reality might best be described as *Webster's* describes it: "that which exists independent of ideas concerning it."

Chapter 12

London, England: Gwennie Scott Agrees to Reveal a Most Wonderful Healing

What I'd seen and heard in Medjugorje had proven most unsettling. The experiences that had been described to me took on all the weight of reality. As far as I was concerned, they existed independently of the doubts, of the "hype," of the hysteria which surrounded them. This quest of mine had ceased to be an amusing adventure.

Gwennie Scott must have sensed the shift in my perceptions. Her first words to me, when I returned to England, were, "Yes, my dear, I'll be glad to see you. Come out tomorrow and we'll talk." At nine the next morning, I eagerly boarded the train for Muswell Hill.

Gwennie stood at the gate, her usual warm, smiling self. She looked even younger than I remembered her, though her steps were still measured and deliberate as she led me through the long, narrow entryway into her house. "I'm all right, my dear," she said, again as if in answer to my question. "Slowing down a bit, but no matter, I keep going."

Gwennie knew immediately why I was so anxious to see her. "So you want to hear about my most remarkable cure, do you?" she said, smiling. "That's what you want to hear, now is it?" I nodded in surprise. I asked her, was I really so transparent? "Well, I think you're ready to hear it now," she answered brusquely.

She began her amazing story.

"Let me start at the beginning. About 17 or 18 years ago, a young man, then in his thirties, was suffering from a miserable condition. As a child, he had always had difficulty with his colon, never eliminating regularly, you see, and was forced to use purging medicines continually. By the time I met him, his colon had lost all peristaltic action, and for years he had been forced to undergo colonic irrigations every two weeks just to survive. His activities had to be carefully planned around these irrigations, and his general health was far from optimal. He was growing increasingly discouraged.

"In desperation, he consulted England's leading gastroenterologist. Finding no muscle tone at all, no peristalsis, in this young man's intestines, the physician suggested, as a last resort, an operation: a section of his colon would be removed and the remainder bound up for a designated period of time. The young man was, however, told that the chances of this helping him were minimal, and that he might be left in worse condition than before. With no more assurance than this, he elected simply to continue the unpleasant and inconvenient irrigations.

"In his travels, he had always had to make certain that he could find a clinic nearby equipped to give him the necessary cleansings. For instance, when his family wintered in Nassau, he was forced to fly to Miami every two weeks for his irrigation. Poor boy, the problem never left his mind."

"How did he happen to know of you?" I asked.

"He didn't," Gwennie answered in her brusque manner, "but I would say that it was meant to be. Some years ago—about 18, it was—I went to a party in Belgrave Square. Oh yes, I was still moving about in those days. There must have been 100 people in the room. Suddenly, a tall young stranger walked right up to me and said, 'I know you!' To my surprise, I answered, 'And I know you!' I didn't understand why I said this. It was just a 'knowing.'

"From that moment on, a friendship developed between us. Eventually, the young man learned of my clairaudient abilities, and one day he appealed to me for help with his distressing handicap. Oddly enough, this was one of the very few times I ever had to go into a trance in order to treat a patient. I don't know why I had to do this, but there it was."

Gwennie was speaking very slowly now as she carefully recalled what had happened. "During that trance, various people came through—from the other side of life, you know. There were different vibrations, different levels. By the time the third treatment had ended, I knew that something remarkable had taken place.

"For the 17 years since that time, this man has never used his colon. He eats perfectly normally, and he has an enormous appetite—but his colon always remains empty and all waste matter is eliminated through the urine. He is the only man in the world whose body functions in this manner."

It's odd, the things that pass through your mind in a moment of shock. I immediately thought of the glowworms in the Waitomo Caves of New Zealand, who are the only members of the animal kingdom born without a mouth or an alimentary canal.

"But how?" I wanted to know. "What had happened?"

"I really don't know myself," Gwennie replied. "But it seemed to me that I understood, while in trance, that henceforth all of his food would be processed through his liver, that the fiber, the non-metabolized sugars, would all be broken down into absorbable forms. Nothing would be left to enter the large colon."

"Then what you did for this young man was literally to change his metabolism!" I exclaimed. "Do you suppose you caused his body to produce a unique enzyme which could break down this residue? Oh, Gwennie, think of the implications!"

Gwennie raised her hands in the air. "Before we think of the implications," she said to me gravely, "don't say 'I,' 'Gwennie,' must have changed him. I might have caused this or that. I'm only a channel. The healing comes from the source of all life."

We talked for awhile about this miracle. "Did the young man immediately realize that something had happened to him?" I asked.

"Well, he later told me that he'd felt a strange feeling of lightness...of a cleansing. But, of course, he couldn't know what had taken place within his body until some days later."

Gwennie told me that the young man had been planning a trip to Venice for the end of the week following her healing. Before leaving London, he went as usual to Sister Allen's clinic for his irrigation treatment. He later told Gwennie that Sister Allen had exclaimed in disbelief, "But what is this? There is absolutely nothing in your colon!"

The young man had been equally stunned. He had originally gone to Gwennie hoping that, through her healing work, peristalsis would be restored to his colon. But now this! Something completely inexplicable was happening, for he had eaten normally ever since he'd paid his visit to Gwennie some days before.

I could imagine the thoughts and the questions that must have been racing through his mind during that trip to Venice. He was probably well aware that the longest a human being can live without eliminating feces is about 108 days. Even if you adhered to a totally liquid diet, there would always be some residue that had to be eliminated; even if the colon were completely removed, this residue would still have to be dealt with by a colostomy bag of some sort.

Anxious to know what was happening inside his body, the young man went for x-rays as soon as he arrived back in England. The radiologist was astounded at what he saw: the totally empty colon of a man who was eating a balanced diet daily, but who nonetheless had experienced no normal elimination or colonic irrigation whatsoever in the course of several weeks.

I returned to London late that evening with little time to change for the large dinner party I was attending. As we dined, my thoughts were far away, back in the quiet room in Muswell Hill where, 17 years before, a miracle had taken place.

I couldn't wait to hear more. I telephoned Gwennie the next morning, hoping my early call wouldn't awaken her. "Do you think it would be possible for me to come back sometime to meet this young man?" I asked her eagerly. "Would it be too great an invasion of his privacy? Is he going to mind your having told me of this?"

Gwennie replied, quite unperturbed: "Well, first, he's not so very young anymore; that was 17 years ago, remember. And he's a very kind person, very intelligent. I can certainly ask him if he'll speak to you and let you know. It may be several weeks before I reach him, though. He's always on the go."

I was about to hang up when Gwennie remarked abruptly: "Wait! There's something else. You must always remember that the basis of all healing is love and compassion. And, of course, true humility."

Chapter 13

Belgrave Square, London: A German Psychic Keeps Her Audience in Suspense

Quite by chance, I learned that the famous German psychic Dorice Hannan was now in London. I reached her by phone, and made an appointment for a time shortly before she was scheduled to return home. I counted myself lucky; I'd been determined to see Dorice Hannan, and this would save me a trip to Germany.

Dorice turned out to be a slim, smartly dressed young woman; you could easily imagine her managing a fashionable boutique in West Berlin. Nothing in her manner suggested her unusual gifts. Dorice told me she'd been born in the village of Reckling Hausen, in Germany, at the end of the Second World War. She'd been a highly sensitive child; but, contrary to the recollections of many psychics, she remembered her early years as happy ones.

It wasn't until she was about 12 that Dorice had begun to feel she was somehow watching herself from the "outside." Her first experience of this had been so frightening it caused her to lose consciousness. By the age of 16, she had become severely depressed. She was beginning to "pick up on" the feelings of distant relatives; and, while still a student at the *gymnasium*, she had experienced astral, or out-of-body, travel. She could "see around" objects, and she was surprised to learn that others did not seem to have this same ability. She was constantly misunderstood by her classmates, and, though she tried desperately to "belong," Dorice never felt that she was accepted by them. In the end, she went into a depression so deep that she unsuccessfully attempted to commit suicide.

This attempt to terminate her life marked the beginning of a new one. Dorice's eyes took on a faraway look as she recounted the amazing thing that had happened to her next. She recalled how she had watched, detached from her body, as the doctors worked over her to save her life. She had felt a presence, and heard a voice saying, "Go back; spare your family."

At that moment Dorice's sanity returned. "I felt as though I had been through a sort of winter of the soul," she told me. The realization came over her that she had to renew herself because she had important work to do. Her mission in life, she was now certain, was to help others through the use of her paranormal powers. It was to this end that Dorice began to probe, through study, thought and meditation, into the workings of the human mind.

She arrived at some interesting if unrelated conclusions. Dorice told me she had sensed intuitively that, "we are all built like magnets, some of us positive, some of us negative." She asserted that, "around 1950, a new breed of children began to appear in the world, and with them a spirit of rebelliousness never before seen in such intensity." She was hopeful that this strange rebelliousness would in the end lead to beneficial changes for humanity.

Though she was married and had a young daughter, Dorice worked tirelessly as a healer. Regarding her healing, she observed: "First, to be well, people must learn to release their emotions." She felt we were all fundamentally good. "The seed is always good, but the soil is often bad. More compassion is needed if the world is to survive," she told me with great earnestness. She warned that too many people "keep themselves emotionally switched off."

Later, I watched as Dorice gave, before a small, keenly attentive audience, what was supposed to be an hour-long demonstration. She channeled "messages from the dead" for the various people seated before her. The messages were obviously hitting the mark; there were tears of recognition from some members of the audience, surprised laughter from others, as the cryptic phrases, meaningful only to particular persons, came through her lips.

The demonstration was going well when suddenly an anxious look came across Dorice's finely sculpted features. She put her hand to her forehead. "Someone is in great distress in your family," she said, pointing to a large middle-aged man in the third row. "They are thinking of suicide, and you must help them!"

The man in question looked vaguely noncommittal. Then he shook his head, as if to indicate a complete lack of identification with the alarming message. Dorice insisted; the man, becoming visibly annoyed, began to shift uneasily in his seat. There was an odd tension growing between the two, which by now even the most obtuse among us could sense.

Dorice reached around suddenly to the back of her head, as if she'd just received a blow. She closed her eyes tightly, then said: "I'm sorry, I can't complete the demonstration. This has disturbed me terribly. Anything I would say from now on, today, I would simply be making up." She stood up and, eyes downcast, walked quickly out of the room.

Dorice's honesty was impressive. We all knew she had come a great distance to make this appearance; but she would not let go of her conviction that someone connected with a member of the audience was facing grave danger, and that conviction had compelled her to break off the séance.

Dorice was a talented painter and writer as well as a sensitive. At the time we met, her latest book, one intended to help people better understand themselves, had just come off the press; she was busily at work on a sequel. You felt this dynamic young woman could have pursued any number of formidable careers with the certainty of success. But she would remind me more than once that, "I've found my mission in life. I can use my sensitivity to help others."

After we'd said good-bye, I was sorry I hadn't questioned Dorice further about her ability to "see around" objects. Did this occur randomly; or could she see around an object whenever she decided to exercise that faculty? If the latter were true, it seemed to me that this constituted unquestionable evidence for the existence of yet another "sense." Architects and surgeons are said to possess a capability for what is called "concrete visualization." Was this the same thing as Dorice possessed? Or could Dorice indeed, by looking at the back of a man's head, actually "see" his face as well? Could this possibly mean that Dorice could see whatever was *in front of* the man—what was for others blocked from view?

I realized once again my quest was no superficial lark.

Dorice Hannan's aborted demonstration of channeling had taken place at No. 33 Belgrave Square, home of the Spiritualist

Association of Great Britain, whose former president and very enthusiastic supporter was Sir Arthur Conan Doyle, famed as the creator of Sherlock Holmes, but equally celebrated as one of the first great researchers into psychic phenomena. The Spiritualist Association's mandate continued to be to search for evidence of personal survival after death. Taking part in this endeavor were psychics who came from all over Europe to channel messages from those who were, in the words of the psychics, "in spirit."

It is generally agreed that spiritualism is significantly more widespread and respected in England than in any other country in the western world, and that the psychic gift is more often accepted and cultivated in England precisely because of this respect. We should always remember, however, that many psychics can seemingly provide information about the dead without using "controls" or "communicators" or "spirit guides." In *A New Approach to Psychical Research*, Anthony Flew suggests that the "climate of opinion in a particular country tends to direct the way in which a psychic will develop." In one environment, the psychic might "become an orthodox spirit medium, in another environment, perhaps a seer or a prophetess, or a 'wise woman.'"

There are, of course, many who believe that spirit mediums merely pick up information about the dead relatives or friends of their clients from the subconscious mind of the client, and don't actually receive messages from the dearly departed.

Isn't such a feat of mind reading in itself an amazing occurrence? The scientists certainly don't want to think so.

The night before I left England, I found myself at a dinner party, seated beside a celebrated British anthropologist who was the holder of many degrees, the author of a dozen books, and, when all was said and done, a scientist of the greatest erudition and wit.

I urged this most distinguished man to attend—even if it were just for the amusement of a single afternoon—a demonstration of channeling at 33 Belgrave Square. "I realize," I said deferentially, "that perhaps the medium isn't really receiving messages from the dead, that perhaps what is taking place is only a form of mind reading. But that, too, is remarkable, don't you think?"

71

He laughed a marvelously deep laugh. "There can't possibly be anything to any of it," he scoffed jovially, "but if there is, then the game's over. With those sorts of wild cards in the deck, we can hang it all up."

What he seemed to be saying was that, if psychic phenomena were a reality, then there would be no point at all to pursuing science. But science had to be pursued—and therefore psychic phenomena could not be a reality! It seemed to me that this marvelously capable anthropologist, with his scholarship, his experience, and his probing mind, should be setting out to find some answers in the face of this evidence rather than ridiculing the question.

Brendan O'Regan, director of research at the Institute of Noetic Sciences, reminds us that, "there are new messenger systems and forms of information transmission being discovered in molecular biology with every passing month." It may be that one day we will find a perfectly simple explanation for what happens at 33 Belgrave Square.

No, the game is not over. The fun has just begun!

During my flight from England to America, I wondered if that celebrated scientist would indeed visit Belgrave Square—as he had finally promised me he would—and whether, if he did, the power of his denying, skeptical thoughts would influence the demonstration in any way. For there can no longer be any doubt about the role the observer plays in the manifestation of *psi* phenomena. We do not yet know on what bands of energy psychic phenomena operate; but we have reason to believe that emotion can be an affecting factor. We all know there is no such thing as an unbiased interview; the interviewer always interacts with the person being interviewed, with each influencing the other—and, the more open and sensitive the persons involved, the more powerful the interaction will be. If the interviewer is at all empathetic, an energy will almost certainly spring up between the two.

By the same token, it's hard not to believe that an even more powerful interaction takes place between the unusually open and sensitive psychic and the researcher who is testing the psychic. In those cases where a psychic is being tested by an unsympathetic or doubt-filled examiner, the energy bands by which paranormal knowledge travels will become weakened and diffused. At some point, we will have to accept that thoughts have energy, and can weaken or be weakened—and the reverse. Many of us have had at least one or two experiences of intuitively 'knowing' something. Multiply these experiences by a thousand and you will perhaps get a sense of what it is like to be a psychic.

The accepted methodologies of modern science may be totally inappropriate for testing certain phenomena. It's encouraging to note that many psychic insights have a physical out-picturing, and that science now has the tools for a possible verification of these out-picturings. A renowned electrical engineer, Bob Beck, once told me that the brain waves of psychics, metaphysical healers and great creative artists and musicians have, in their "moment of inspiration," the same electromagnetic frequencies as those which emanate from the earth: 7.83 hertz. The length of the "moment" may be only seconds, but it seems that in that flash of time a connection is made with another dimension; a whole symphony may pour forth within a composer's brain—or a detailed vision of the past and future may blaze its way into the consciousness of a psychic.

We can certainly agree with the editor of *Nature* magazine, John Maddox, when he warns us that, "extraordinary caution should be exerted when confronted with data that appears to fly in the face of not only basic common sense, but also a great deal of physics and chemistry as they are presently understood." Caution, yes; unquestioning rejection or indifference, no! Because a phenomenon cannot be explained in the light of our present understanding, why should we assume that it cannot be explained in the light of future knowledge? Do we really believe all the doors have been opened, all of the universe's laws discovered, all nature's secrets divulged?

Could the sounds of a radio have been explained in the light of the knowledge extant in 200 B.C.? The laws of aerodynamics existed long before birds evolved able to make use of them. What would the reaction of our cave ancestors have been to the sight of a supersonic jet in the sky? The laws of symphonic harmony existed long before music itself emerged in man's evolving brain.

If the past, the present, and the future do exist simultaneously, as the clairvoyant gift suggests, there must be as yet unrecognized laws by which certain individuals are made *conscious* of this amazing fusion of time.

Might not those quiet, non-exploitative psychic healers have contacted a band of energy that science has not yet identified? Perhaps psychic healers herald the next step in our evolution. This possibility presents us with a wholly different game, one in which we're all novices, with everything to learn. Can a blind man prove or disprove a sighted man's description of a sunset?

My long journey home was almost completed; a voice over the loudspeaker was announcing our descent. Gwennie Scott's words were still echoing in my ears: "For 17 years, this man has not used his colon." Had the E-coli bacteria in the colon been permanently destroyed? Had this man's digestive enzymes undergone a mutation enabling them to destroy all semi-solid residue? If this were so, might this mutation be chemically duplicatable; might it enable the same digestive process to take place in the bodies of other human beings?

Imagine a colon cancer victim, dependent on a colostomy bag for life, suddenly freed! Could we not use this technology in space travel, where the accumulating feces of the astronaut were a constant concern? Why hadn't anyone in the medical field made an effort to understand what had been going on in this man's body for 17 years? Wouldn't this dramatic demonstration of Gwennie Scott's paranormal powers constitute irrefutable proof of *psi*? My thoughts raced wildly on.

Gwennie had said it might take some time to track down the young man.

I still didn't even know his name!

Chapter 14

Atlanta, Georgia: Spirit Doctors or Multiple Personality Disorder?

Back in Atlanta now, I paid a visit to a very attractive woman named Sally Vickers whom I'd heard practiced the art of psychic healing in a way quite different from any I'd yet encountered. Sally called herself an "etheric healer," and she worked on the assumption that each of us had an etheric body that registered any illness or abnormality taking place in the physical body. She believed that a healing of the etheric body would extend healing to the physical body.

I found Sally living north of Atlanta, in a sunny apartment filled with plants, cats, crystals and an odd collection of pyramids of obscure and intriguing origin. Sally was slim and almost fragile-looking, with a kind of attenuated beauty; to this was added a voice of surprising authority. Her dedication to her work shone through as she set about explaining to me, with care and cogency, her unusual methodology.

She began her treatment by inviting the subject to lie down in a comfortable and relaxed manner on a narrow table. The room was dimly lit, with soothing music playing in the background; all of this was calculated, I assumed, to put the subject at ease.

Sally then went into a deep trance, and, starting at the head, "read" the etheric body of the client down through the feet, pointing out areas of weakness, disease or injury as she went along. Those who had been so treated attested to her consistent accuracy. She then called on various "spirit doctors" who, she said, "placed" healing needles—or healing crystals, depending on the nature of the problem—in the afflicted areas. Then the subject was given detailed advice on the future care of his or her health. Sometimes, an individual diet was prescribed.

The session lasted less than an hour and, if needles had been "placed" in the shoulder area, for instance, the subject was warned not to raise the arms for several hours, as this would cause pain. The subject was further reminded that post-treatment caution was extremely important.

Sally contended that, "Many people do not know or realize that it is in the etheric that the correction of any disharmony is first manifested. The subconscious mind plays the all-important role in both disease and in its cure, and, if the etheric double can 'accept' this, then there will be a healing." Sally's diagnostic abilities were alone worth serious study, and I ended up leaving her sunny apartment with many unanswered questions.

As I drove back to town, I recalled a lecture I had once attended given by Christine Cosner Sizemore, whose much-publicized manifestation of multiple personalities had brought worldwide attention to the syndrome when her autobiography, *The Three Faces of Eve*, was published in 1957.

In her lecture, Ms. Sizemore had revealed that when she was manifesting one of her personalities she was myopic and needed glasses. When she was manifesting another, her vision was perfect. In one personality, she suffered from arthritis; when she switched to another, she became completely pain-free.

The question had been asked of the lecturer whether psychic healing might simply be a form of hypnosis. It seemed to me that, if this were so, hypnotism needed to be investigated with as much vigor as is applied to the testing of pharmaceuticals. Ms. Sizemore said, however, that viruses such as the cold or flu virus would always make the transition from one personality to another. If she was suffering from flu symptoms in one, she would suffer from flu symptoms in another.

I was sorry I hadn't asked Sally Vickers whether her particular mode of healing was successful with viruses. I'd heard that some psychic healers could induce a fever in the subject, and that the fever would then rid the body of the virus. As my search continued, the powers of the mind were taking on a greater and greater fascination for me.

Some people have suggested that "spirit guides" or "spirit doctors," and the like, merely represent the surfacing of another personality of the person in trance, a personality to which there is normally no access in the waking state. More questions and fewer answers.

The very word "spirit" defies concrete definition. Many outstanding seers and prophets have never referred to "spirits." From whence, then, come their illuminations? Do mediums suspected of working only from the reptilian brain exhibit scale frequencies different from those of the earth and those of healers and mediums of a 'higher order'—the "7.83 hertz crowd," as I've come to call them? Perhaps, one day, medical science will know how to apply a certain frequency and thereby draw forth the corresponding spirit—and bring about what used to be called a "miraculous" cure.

Chapter 15

Dunwoody, Georgia:
A Psychic Sleuth for All Seasons

It was early one morning, and I was headed south to Dunwoody, in Georgia, to keep an appointment with a young woman who was helping the police investigate a murder case.

From the accounts I'd read of murder in general, I was betting the assailant was young.

Murder is seldom committed by the elderly. There aren't any statistics to back this up, but certainly the passions abate as one grows older. The act of murder must surely take a lot of psychological energy, and the elderly don't appear to get all that worked up. Aggression seems to be tied up with certain hormones; passion and personal vendettas aside, we don't hear of golden age hit men committing acts of violence. Who would hire an elderly killer, one usually with shaky hands and poor eyesight?

These irrelevant considerations ran through my mind as I pulled into the driveway belonging to the attractive brick house of Phyllis Williams O'Neal, one of the South's best-known psychics.

Phyllis stated early in our conversation that three out of four persons had at least some degree of psychic ability: "It's like a new language you must learn to recognize and understand," she declared.

I asked her how her gift had first become manifest.

She replied, "When I was three, there were two deaths in my family. I remember being a highly emotional child; following these deaths, I began to have dreadful nightmares.

"My paternal grandmother and aunt had some psychic ability, but no one talked about it, since metaphysics was an area looked upon with great suspicion by my mother's side of the family. I secretly harbored a nagging curiosity about the entire subject, and would sometimes slip away and visit clairvoyants. When my own random insights began to occur with increasing frequency, I tried to suppress them at first; but finally, in my early thirties, I told my family about them. From that time on, I began to use my insights—or 'illuminations'—to help others."

I wondered how she knew when she was having an 'illumination?' Phyllis answered that she felt a strong pressure on the left side of her brain. It was a very definite sensation. When she gave a reading, she asked her subjects what questions they wanted answered; but, if necessary, she could 'read' for people who spoke no English, picking up their thoughts telepathically. She then induced a state of self-hypnosis—she didn't use the word "trance"—and let the answers come through. "I get into a man's head as easily as into a woman's, and I understand the differences in their thought processes. The work can be draining, though, for you're picking up other people's aches, pains and sorrows."

Phyllis explained that when she was giving a reading she asked for the session to be taped, since she herself was in a hypnotic state at the time and completely unaware of what was being said. The tape could be replayed later, at the subject's leisure, so that no nuance would be missed.

She told me that she often received uninvited random feelings about the world in general. She saw much violence and sorrow, but she was hopeful that the human race was progressing. Curious about the murder case she'd mentioned when I'd called for an appointment, I asked her how she'd become involved.

She began by describing to me how, one warm August evening, an attractive young woman named Susan, buyer for a large department store, had been found murdered in the living room of her newly remodeled house. Earlier that evening, Susan had invited friends over for a house-warming; when they arrived, they had found Susan's lifeless body lying on the bloodstained carpet. Nothing in the house had been disturbed. There was no apparent motive. A desperate struggle had preceded her death, that was certain. The killer had evidently worn gloves, for there were no fingerprints.

A friend of the victim remembered that many months earlier she and Susan had gone to Phyllis O'Neal for a reading. She remembered that Phyllis always taped her readings, and that, in a trance state at the time, Phyllis would have no recollection of what had been said; a tape of that reading had to be somewhere in Susan's house. The concerned friend approached police with this information. A search of Susan's desk drawers yielded up the tape.

Phyllis had told Susan in the course of the reading that she 'saw' a metallic gray sports car, and that its owner was "dangerous" and would do her "bodily harm." The police listened intently to the contents of the tape. Then they paid a visit to Phyllis. They had decided not to tell her what the tape had revealed, or that they were now actually seeking on the strength of the reading the owner of a metallic gray sports car. As though hearing her words for the first time, Phyllis listened intently to the recording of the session. When the gray sports car was mentioned, the police investigator stopped the tape and asked her if she could 'see' who was driving the car. Phyllis stared at the opposite wall in concentration. Suddenly, there flashed before her eyes the same sports car. Inside it, she could partially see the figure of an expensively dressed young man.

"I couldn't make out anything more than that," Phyllis told me. "I couldn't 'see' his face, but he seemed to be wearing designer blue jeans, expensive clothes—but that was all I could 'see.'" Phyllis promised to call me when she had more followup information.

Even though I remained in the States for some while, I heard nothing further from Phyllis. Months later, I learned that her beloved husband, ill for so long, had died. Knowing how devastated she must be, I called immediately. She seemed anxious to talk about her loss.

"My certainty that death is a natural transition has helped me a great deal with my sorrow," she began, "and I do believe that my particular gift enabled me to guide him at the end. He was in such pain. I would guide him into past-life regressions, and the pain would cease during those periods of time. This tells you something about the nature of pain, doesn't it? And about the power of the mind.

"In his last days, he was in and out of a coma. One of the doctors finally said to me, 'You've got to release him.' So, the following day, I told my husband, 'The next time you see the tunnel with the white light, if it is your soul's purpose, you must go on and not look back at me.' His answer will always remain with me. He whispered, 'If I do leave, it will only be my intellect telling me to go.'"

Phyllis quickly changed the subject to her work. "Work is a wonderful antidote for sorrow," she commented. "I'm writing a book now, and suddenly I seem to have more clients than I can handle. I'm busy every single day except Sunday. So much has happened since we last talked that I haven't had time to find out how the murder case I spoke about was finally resolved. But, wait; here, I can give you the telephone number of poor Susan's best friend, the one who told the police about the tape of my reading. You might want to call her and see if she's heard anything."

I found out Susan's friend had moved to Florida. After several unsuccessful attempts, I was finally able to reach her early one morning. It seemed she had indeed been very close to Susan, but shortly after Susan's death she herself had suffered a near-fatal illness, a ruptured appendix.

"Incidentally," she added, "my illness had been predicted by Phyllis; only she said it would happen in ten years, and instead it happened in ten months. Phyllis told me she 'saw' the number ten, and since I looked so healthy at the time she assumed the illness was ten years away. In any event, I've had a long, hard recovery, and I've been forced to give up my job and come to Florida so my parents can take care of me. Through all this, I've lost touch with the investigation of Susan's murder. It hadn't been solved when I left Georgia, and I have no idea where her mother and father are now; at one time, they were living somewhere in the Midwest. I really don't know who could tell you."

My next call was to the District Attorney's office; giving Susan's full name, I learned that her murder remained unsolved, an "open case." Without witnesses or clues, the likelihood of police ever finding the killer were slim. Did the metallic gray sports car exist? We know only one thing: Phyllis O'Neal accurately saw Susan "in danger" and likely to suffer "bodily harm."

Chapter 16

Mexico City and the Exorcising Power of Eggs

I had been planning a trip to Mexico for late January to visit once again the Spanish colonial town of San Miguel de Allende. What a wonderful opportunity this would be, I'd thought, to talk to a certain healer in Mexico City I'd heard of, an old woman said to effect astonishing cures.

There was a problem, though. No one could quite remember the woman's name. A French friend in San Marlo did manage to come up with a telephone number, and somebody else had an address they thought might be the healer's daughter's. But this was not a great deal to go on, to be sure. I dialed the number many times from the U.S., but all lines to Mexico City appeared to be *no contestan*—no answer—or *occupado*—busy—or *no funciona*—not working.

The whole project seemed to be on the verge of collapse.

On the morning I was scheduled to leave, I woke up with a burning head and a miserably sore throat. But all the plans had been made, and I was determined to go. Besides, a delightful friend had agreed to come from Monterey to act as my interpreter. Flavio Munez had served in the Mexican embassies in Washington and London and spoke impeccable English. In addition, he had an easy charm that I felt would help me extract information from the aging healer.

When we met in Mexico City that evening, Flavio tried the all-important telephone number repeatedly. He was told, "The *senora* who heals has gone"—but in a tone he described as "highly unconvincing." He telephoned me next morning to say he'd tried again, and this time had been informed—the voice of the informer growing ever more brusque— that, "The *senora* who heals has gone away for good!"

You might have thought this would be a cause for pessimism. But not for Flavio. "I think she is there," he told me excitedly. "Let us take a chance and go to the daughter's address."

The Return of Female Prophetic Power in Our Time

I was feeling worse than the day before, and I longed to beg off from this whole expedition. But Flavio had come so far to help me that I couldn't really refuse his enthusiastic offer. He appeared at my hotel; I leaned heavily on his arm as we made our way slowly toward the taxi. Perhaps my sore throat beclouded my judgement, but I was absolutely certain that the address was all a mistake.

We drove for miles through storm-clouds of exhaust fumes, assailed on every side by blaring horns and traffic that threatened to annihilate us. We finally reached the farthest limits of Mexico City's suburbs. We took a wrong turn three times; an extremely spirited conversation erupted between our taxi driver and another; our driver suddenly slammed on the brakes, turned off the meter, and pointed triumphantly toward a house.

This was indeed the address—or, at least, the right number was painted in big black numerals on the high wall surrounding a very small cement courtyard. The plaster house behind the wall was tightly shuttered against the morning sun. We rang; a woman wrapped in a heavy black shawl quickly appeared at the gate. Her greeting was warm and inviting—till we mentioned the *senora* who heals.

"No, no," she murmured, lips tightening, "the *senora* is not here." Her smile had abruptly faded to a frown. "She's gone...She's gone to...She's gone to Guadalajara!" I was sure the gatekeeper had pulled the name *Guadalajara* out of the blue, probably thinking the town was far enough away to discourage further inquiries on our part.

Flavio was not so easily put off. "But the American only wants to speak to her briefly," he explained cajolingly. "She is writing a book on women with psychic and healing powers." Now the woman's eyes took on a frightened look. "No, no, no, you cannot see the *senora*; she isn't here anymore," she implored us. "She's gone away, she's in Guadalajara." Still repeating her original story, she slammed the iron-grille door shut and retreated quickly across the tiny courtyard back into the plaster house.

Flavio was still unconvinced. Over my protests, he headed for a nearby telephone booth and called the number again. This time, he received a rapid-fire lecture from a staccato voice which apparently belonged to the healer's daughter. "No! Mama is not here, she's gone," came the volley of agitated words (or so he reported to me afterward). "She's never coming back. The last time she was written up in a book, her life became impossible. People from everywhere brought their sick to the house! She couldn't breathe...She's left...She's not coming back...Don't call anymore!" There was silence at the other end of the line.

Flavio finally hung up. He was still certain Mama was hiding inside that plaster house. But he was equally certain we would never reach her.

I was perfectly happy to give it all up and crawl back to my hotel. My head was throbbing and my entire body ached. But Flavio had a tenacity that I could never have suspected. Now, to my amazement, he rushed to the corner kiosk and bought an armful of newspapers, each one of which he proceeded to thoroughly peruse. I shook my head stenuously. "No, no, you don't understand," I admonished him. "Not just *anyone*, Flavio. Not someone who advertises in the newspapers!"

He didn't seem to hear me. He rapidly read off the names of fortunetellers, tea leaf readers, astrologers; all of them seemed to be located in towns miles from Mexico City. Finally, Flavio came across a particularly flamboyant advertisement which read *Psychic Readers and Healers*. This conglomeration of psychics was apparently to be found in Mexico City, at a place called "The Tarot Cafe." Flavio suggested we go there immediately. I quickly demurred. "Let's join your wife and have lunch," I begged, "let's go to the Anthropological Museum, let's go *anywhere*..."

"No, no, you must talk to someone!" insisted Flavio. He was caught up in the spirit of the chase! Before I could protest any further, we were in a taxi again and retracing our route at a giddying pace through the outskirts of the city; before I knew it, we were back in the center of town, plunging forward through the heavily congested streets. We finally slammed to a stop in front of the street number of the mysterious, highly self-touted "Tarot Cafe."

The building was singularly unprepossessing. At the sight of it, even the ebullient Flavio was disheartened.

But, since we'd come this far, we reluctantly made our way inside. This wasn't easy, and involved climbing four dreary flights of stairs, till at last we stood before a small brown door upon which were printed, in very faded letters, the words "Tarot Cafe."

We entered a small anteroom.

To someone who seemed to be in charge, Flavio laboriously explained our mission. He very carefully emphasized that, "No, we don't want a reading. We only want to interview one of the psychics."

Even as he spoke, we both felt this adventure was sure to be a waste of time.

We were led through the diminutive anteroom into an even smaller room. It reeked of incense and was illuminated by a single tube of blue neon light. An array of burning candles gave off the thin odor of synthetic perfume. Flavio and I exchanged amused glances. On narrow tables along the walls stood cheap plastic replicas of Buddha, of Vishnu, and of Hanuman-Shiva, side-by-side with a tattered assortment of Catholic saints; above this disparate lot hung crude drawings of the signs of the Zodiac and the Third Eye. I seem to remember a Christmas tree standing in one corner, strung with tattered silver tinsel; but I can't be sure.

Seated at a small table in the center of the room was a very young woman. This woman—she was practically a girl—had the high sharp cheekbones of an Andean Indian. She gazed at us with large dark eyes which spoke of infinite sadness. I forgot the ridiculous surroundings of the room in the sudden rush of sympathy I felt for this girl who, scarcely more than a child, was mechanically shuffling a worn deck of cards.

Flavio explained to her that he would ask her questions about her life and translate the answers into English; the American lady would take it down for a book she was writing about female psychics. The girl nodded in assent and put away her cards. The interview began. And, starting from that very moment, she stared at me steadily until the end of the interview. Why was she staring at me? I wondered. I would understand why only after I got back to my hotel.

The young girl's name was Elvia Margoth Chaquinga Zurita. She had been born near Quito, in the mountains of Ecuador, and was one of many children of a very large Catholic family. She spoke with dignity of her parents' struggle to care for them and of her grandfather's power to heal—a power that she believed she had inherited.

"Tell me how your grandfather effected his cures," I asked.

"It is a gift from God," she answered quietly. Elvia described how, when she was a small child, she had watched in awe as the diseased were brought into the presence of her grandfather for a healing. First, he would pray; then, he would take a fresh egg and pass it slowly along the patient's body. All of a sudden, the patient would feel well. Her grandfather would break open the egg, and, "the inside of the egg would have turned black."

I looked inquiringly at Flavio. Yes, he indicated, I had understood correctly. Elvia continued. When she was about ten, she had come upon a small, terrified boy, and she had wanted to help him somehow. "Remembering my grandfather, I quickly found an egg and passed it over the trembling child. He immediately became calm. Then I felt a brilliant light inside me, and I knew that I, too, had the healing power."

When she got older, Elvia moved to Mexico City. Now people came to her at the fourth floor Tarot Cafe, paid her a handful of pesos, and were either healed or had their problems solved or had their futures read.

"How do your predictions come to you?" I asked.

Elvia explained that, first, she went into a state of deep concentration. Then, "when I feel a coldness within me, I know I am receiving the vibrations of insights and not simply the thoughts of my own imagination."

Elvia had always led a lonely life. She had few friends in Mexico City. She described herself as a "very private person inside." She was extremely sensitive to the suffering of others; she wanted to help them whenever she could. People came to her with money problems, they came to her with family problems, they came to her with physical problems. She could often identify the kind of problem that existed without being told; then she would set about resolving it.

She got very involved in her work, Elvia told us, and felt that this work had enabled her to grow spiritually. She voiced deep sadness at the state of the world, and expressed the belief that humankind must evolve to a higher level if it wanted to survive. Her big sad eyes became even graver as she declared to us finally, "We are destroying ourselves. We are destroying ourselves."

The hour was finished. We rose to go. Looking around at the four pitiful walls, I wondered sadly what the rest of Elvia's life would be. Would she ever know anything more than a room like this? Would there ever be any beauty or lightness of humor to gladden those big sad eyes?

I went down the stairs slowly, unable to shake off the peculiar feeling that, along with the interview, something else—something I couldn't explain—had taken place in that garish little room. By the time we reached the hotel, I knew what it was. My forehead was cool; my throat no longer ached. I turned to Flavio. "I'm completely well," I told him quietly. "Do you suppose that Senorita Elvia...?"

I didn't need to finish my sentence. I understood now what Elvia's steady gaze into my eyes all through the interview had been about. After we'd left, had she broken open an egg? Had the interior been black?

I would never know—but I would never cease to wonder.

Chapter 17

Tierra Del Fuego, Argentina:
Drawn to the South Pole's Ambit

Some say the poles have an influence on clairvoyant abilities; there are no theories as to how. Polar influence or no, I was glad to be visiting Tierra del Fuego, that cold and windy archipelago, half-Chilean, half-Argentinian, that is roughly the same distance from the South Pole as the Alaskan Panhandle is from the North. I was happy to have the opportunity of meeting, here in the legendary city of Ushuaia, a psychic named Violetta Susa.

It was a wet and extremely cold day with a sharp biting wind blowing in from the sea, when I eagerly set out to find this noted clairvoyant. You could hardly believe it was summer; the seasons are, of course, reversed in Tierra del Fuego, and I knew that one day soon these muddy streets would be deep in snow. I finally arrived, numb and shivering, at the address I'd been given: the very last house in the Calle San Martin in that slumbering old seaside city of Ushuaia.

I learned from the young man whose shop faced Violetta's studio that she'd gone away for the weekend; I would have to come back on Monday. Not wishing to brave the cold again quite so immediately, I asked him to tell me something about her.

His face brightened. "Oh, she's quite remarkable," he happily declared. "Many, many people come to see her. I can give you an example of something interesting that happened to me personally. Recently, while driving to Buenos Aires, I had an accident. When I got back, Violetta met me with the words: 'You had an accident, didn't you? I "saw" it.' Then she proceeded to tell me where the accident had taken place, the exact time of day, and even the make of the car that had hit me. I've never known anyone like her!"

The following Monday proved to be a beautiful day, with clear skies and much warmer weather. The mountaintops and glaciers surrounding the bay glittered in the morning sunlight. I hastened to the Calle San Martin. After I had waited in her house for about an hour, Violetta made her entrance.

I was immediately taken by her large, expressive eyes which seemed to widen whenever she spoke. Short black hair framed her arrestingly attractive face, and her manner of speech conveyed a strange and unusual energy and intensity.

"What happens when people come to you for a reading?" I asked.

"Generally, I use the Tarot cards—but I use them only to help me concentrate, to sharpen my focus. It is not so much of a random thing with me. I am pretty well able to control it. I can call it up when I want to use it; then I begin to 'see' things, pictures. I am very honest. I always tell subjects exactly what I see; then I try to help them, to show them ways in which they can best use the information. I also do some healing, using my hands to alleviate pain. I make many cures."

"When did your talent first emerge?"

"I was a very sad person when I was around the age of 16. Both my parents died within three years of each other, and this was a very difficult time for me. Yes, I can tell you more precisely when it started. My father and I were dining alone one evening, when suddenly he fell forward. His face landed in the plate he had been eating from. He was gone! It was a terrible shock. I had my first—how shall I describe it?—experience, shortly after that. Strangely enough, I have never been frightened by these clairvoyant experiences. I simply accept them. I don't understand this thing I have, but I believe it is something quite formidable."

"Then you are aware of the tremendous importance of a gift such as yours?"

"Yes." She repeated her words, this time with emphasis. "It is something quite formidable."

"Were there any others in your family who had the same ability?"

"Oh, yes. My father was very telepathic. He could pick up other people's thoughts. I rather think it is somehow hereditary."

We both fell silent for a moment. I looked across the tranquil waters of the bay at the majestic mountains climbing up from its shores. It occurred to me that this must be the exact same scene of unmarred beauty as had greeted those first nomadic tribes who came here so many thousands of years ago. Here, at the bottom of the world, nothing had changed. Such beauty evoked a feeling of permanence; I almost hesitated to shatter the feeling when I asked my final question.

"Violetta, what do you see for the future of the world?"

A deep frown creased her well-shaped brow. She slowly shook her head. "Very bad. Very bad. But after much destruction mankind will 'elevate'—is that the word?—to a higher state. He *must*."

Our interview was at an end.

Chapter 18

Atlanta, Georgia:
The Clairvoyant Who Sensed the Essences of People

On my return to Atlanta, I was invited to a dinner in honor of a well-known horticulturist who was in town to add luster to a flower show scheduled to open the following day. The guests were for the most part out-of-town exhibitors attending the show with their spouses; all were completely unknown to the hostess. The seating arrangement, then, could only have been by chance.

I drew as a dinner partner an exhibitor's youthful husband. He told me he'd recently abandoned the ministry to pursue a doctorate in philosophy. He added casually, "I used to have quite an interest in psychic phenomena."

I was bemused. There was no reason for him to have mentioned this; it wasn't really relevant to his being a minister or seeking a Ph.D in philosophy. I wondered why out of 19 other possibilities I'd ended up sitting next to this particular person.

I confided in him my interest in the paranormal. He immediately replied, "Well, I suppose you've already talked to Hillary Ellers. Now, *she's* a true sensitive."

Coincidence or not, this was how I first became aware of a most courageous young woman, with a most remarkable psychic gift, though several days were to elapse before I could finally catch up with her.

What do we mean when we say that someone is a "sensitive?" There are many sensitive people who are not clairvoyant. A celebrated philosopher once remarked, "There are only two races of men, the sensitive and the insensitive." If this is so, shouldn't we devise a way to test for sensitivity in early childhood, so that all those with a high degree of this quality, psychic or not, can somehow be housed and educated together? Perhaps this is where segregation may legitimately be practiced; in this way, the sensitives of the world would be protected from the push and pull of the heedless and the constant bombardment of trite ideas and mean-ingless clichés. The sensitive ones would create a world of their own, one where they would no longer be trampled on, exploited—even brutalized, as is sometimes the case. An entire loftier species might emerge.

Intellect and courage are found to an equal degree in the sensi-tive and the insensitive alike; all other things being equal, wouldn't we all be better off in a world led by the sensitives?

Particular sensitivities vary widely. I have a friend who is highly sensitive to spatial configurations. She once told me she became vaguely jittery in low ceilinged rooms, and that extremely low ceil-ings had a distinctly dizzying effect on her. If she really wanted to put herself into a panic, she told me, she only had to reread Edgar Allen Poe's *The Cask of Amontillado*, where the unfortunate hero is incarcerated in a narrow space between two walls while still alive. She'd pointed out to me that schizophrenics were sometimes helped by a change in the design of the spaces they occupied—particu-larly overhead spaces.

My friend also confided to me that once, when she was in a cave in Spain where her head nearly brushed the roof, she'd found herself suddenly short of breath. It hadn't been a feeling of claus-trophobia that was causing this panic, she insisted, but something equally disturbing—though she didn't know what. Once she'd descended to the higher ceilinged chambers of the lower caves, the feeling had ceased. This had made me wonder if sensitivity to over-head space might not have contributed to early man's desire to escape from the caves. Were we "hard-wired" one way or the other? Was the sensitivity of the sensitives genetic? On the evidence of the sensitives I'd interviewed so far, the trait did seem to run in families.

In the case of the soft-spoken, gentle Hillary Ellers, it seemed that a troubled home rather than a nurturing environment had been the unlikely catalyst in the development of her particular form of sensitivity. This sensitivity had flowered despite what she characterized as a tragically "dysfunctional" family; perhaps it had somehow flowered *because* of it.

Hillary told me she'd had a difficult childhood, one full of scarring trauma which even now she found it difficult to discuss. Because she had been so unhappy, she began to lead what she called an "interior life." She became deeply religious, and could remember seeing 'visions' and having a sense of 'knowing;' this latter experience didn't seem so odd to her when she learned that all four of her greatgrandmothers had been psychic healers.

When she was 24, Hillary had had an experience that changed her life dramatically. In the middle of one day, she suddenly felt her hair stand on end; then a chill swept over her and an odd sense of powerfulness filled her body. She could remember experiencing lights going on and off, objects shifting around—and the feeling that something, someone, was trying to communicate with her.

Not long after she'd had this strange experience, Hillary went to Florida on vacation. She met a woman there who told her, "You have taken this trip to meet me." The woman turned out to be well-known psychic Ann Nanser, who had immediately recognized in Hillary an unusual gift.

Ann Nanser told the shy young woman it was important that she develop her psychic abilities. The Florida psychic urged Hillary to join a group that practiced meditation. As a sort of test, on the first day the group's director asked Hillary to concentrate on one of the other members of the group and describe what she 'saw.' Hillary found she was able to provide specific information about this total stranger, information far beyond the possibility of a lucky guess. The director then informed Hillary that she was a highly gifted psychic and should set to work to develop her gift.

"I resisted the idea at first," Hillary said with a laugh. "I was afraid I would be considered a witch. I didn't even want to think about it. I tried to deny it."

Lacking the education required for a career in another field— and, as she modestly put it, "having no other particular skills"— Hillary ultimately decided to develop her inborn capacity for psychic 'viewing.' Studying diligently with Anne Hanser for seven years, she mastered the art of meditation. She later studied Cabala under a master named Leroy Zenke.

Cabala! I hadn't heard that word for years. Hillary told me that the Cabalists believe that God is present in all things and thus that everything is analogous to everything else. It is an interesting philosophy, and I could see how its study might help to promote the next step forward in the development of clairvoyance, insofar as clairvoyance presupposes the interrelatedness of all objects and persons as they impinge upon one another, and even seems to provide us with a glimpse of an overall plan.

Hillary told me that the study of the Cabala had only recently been opened to women.

Through the use of these disciplines, Hillary had developed her innate clairvoyance, learning at the same time the techniques of metaphysical healing. Given her sensitivity and her love of people, she had found her life's work.

"But your gift is a natural one," I protested.

"Yes. But, like all natural gifts, it can be improved and fine-tuned through discipline and study. All of us have this gift to some extent; some, of course, have it more than others. But certainly anyone willing to dedicate time and energy to its development can raise it to a higher level."

Hillary's deep religious convictions had grown over the years. "I begin every reading with a prayer and an acknowledgement that my gift is God-given," she told me quietly. "Then I close my eyes, and the answers come."

"What form do they come in?" I asked. "Do you see visions? Hear voices?"

"No," she said, "I seldom see visions. It's mostly just a knowing. If you yourself, for instance, know that a friend of yours has three children, you don't necessarily 'see' those three children in your mind whenever you recall that information. When I do see visions, though, they are always in vivid color rather than in black and white."

According to her many clients, Hillary had a remarkable capacity for sensing the 'essence' of a person—the essence of the person who was present, or the essence of the person who was being asked about. Thanks to this unusual facet of her gift, Hillary was in constant demand by psychotherapists. They often sent her patients for readings; the readings were taped and would be studied later by the therapist. Prior knowledge of a patient's essence saved the therapist many long hours of analytic probing to uncover the true identity of the patient.

Listening to Hillary, I reflected on how often we have asked ourselves, "Who am I *really?*" We wonder, are we amalgams of coping mechanisms? Overcompensations for self-perceived inadequacies? Robot responses to aberrant prenatal influences? Echoes of our parents? Shadows? Sleepwalkers acting out hypnotic commands from a subconscious programmed by long-forgotten conditioning? Are our thoughts and actions decisively influenced by chemical balances or imbalances in our bodies? Are our emotions at the mercy of glandular secretions? At the mercy of soothing or disturbing frequencies in the atmosphere? Of sunspots?

Somewhere deep within each of us, there lies a unique self. Sensing this unique self was Hillary Ellers's special gift. So successful had she become at this sensing that she was now working with more than 100 psychotherapists and holding workshops to help them make optimal use of the information she was able to give them about their patients.

"When you are giving a reading, do you have any physical sensations?" I asked.

"Yes," she answered, "I feel a sort of...how shall I put it?...lightheadedness. I also feel as though I'm working from *way back* in my mind, and that my voice is projected in front. I know this sounds hard to believe, but it's as though I'm reaching back into some deep recess I wouldn't ordinarily have access to. And, yes, there are strange physical sensations or feelings around my head."

Hillary was totally non-judgmental, realizing that each one of us sees life from a different perspective. The suffering in her own childhood had given her a rare understanding of human foibles. She told me she spent less time on physical healings now, having decided to concentrate on the 'readings,' as she called them. "If we could heal the mind itself," she mused. "If we could just teach a person to observe his or her own thinking..."

After the interview, I spent the rest of the day puzzling over those strange sensations Hillary said she had experienced—lights going on and off, objects seeming to move around—after which she had never been the same again. Could this have been some form of the kundalini at work? Dr. Lee Sannella, in his definitive work on the subject, *The Kundalini Experience: Psychosis or Transcendence?* tells us that the Sanskrit word *kundalini* means "she who is coiled," and that it refers to a form of psychospiritual energy that lies dormant in everyone. According to Dr. Sannella, if the kundalini is activated, a powerful stream of psychic energy apparently rises from the base of the spine to the head. This rising is usually accompanied by odd sensations of light. Dr. Sannella asserts that when this happens consciousness is able to "transcend normal limits." There can be a total realization of this energy release, or only a partial one. In either case, it can be a frightening experience, if not understood.

Perhaps it was this that Hillary Ellers experienced, and that had enabled the flowering of her remarkable powers.

Chapter 19

The Psychic from Kent, England Who Foresaw the Lockerbie Air Disaster

"PSYCHIC SAW TUBE CRASH!"

Bold black headlines like these, screaming off the pages of British newspapers, were just one more reminder of the daunting psychic powers of Daphne Possee. According to the news reports, the medium from Kent, England, had correctly predicted the approximate section of the London Underground's District Line—near Richmond Hill—where the 'tube,' or subway, crash of September 18, 1987, would take place, and had even predicted the exact way the train's front carriage would smash headlong into the buffers and leap over them.

Daphne Possee was also credited with having predicted, three years before it happened, the March 6, 1987 ferry disaster off Belgium's busy Zeebrugge Harbor, when the *Herald of Free Enterprise* capsized and 130 people lost their lives. It was said that during her flash of premonition, Daphne clearly heard the word "enterprise," followed by the words "Maidstone Police Station." Even at the time of the ferry disaster when she realized she had foretold it, the last three words seemed odd to the Kent clairvoyant; it wasn't until a few years later that she learned that at the time of the disaster all inquiries in Britain regarding passenger survival were directed to Maidstone Police Headquarters.

Daphne Possee also foretold the bombing of Pan Am Flight 103, over Lockerbie, Scotland, in 1988, and the outbreak of the Persian Gulf War in 1991. In numerous TV interviews, she correctly predicted the Gulf War would last only six weeks. Daphne accurately foretold the outcome of a number of individual elections in the British General Election of 1990; these latter predictions alone won her a permanent place in the hearts of the British tabloid press.

Since Daphne had made a name for herself in Britain, and seemed to have become something of a fixture there, it came as a surprise to me to learn that this popular British psychic had decided to come to the U.S. for a year. More importantly, she would be living in Atlanta during that year! A leading Atlanta newspaper carried the story, adding that the famed psychic would be appearing at a local theater on a particular evening and would demonstrate her remarkable skills before a sizable audience.

I could hardly wait!

The night of the appearance came, and...

I'm not sure what I'd been expecting, but it was certainly not the glamorous blond in the beaded red dress who stepped smartly out into the footlights. I found her appearance somehow disturbing. She drew the microphone close to her mouth, tossed back her gleaming hair, exhibited all the flair and presence of a seasoned performer— except for her eyes. Daphne Possee's eyes were large and penetrating, but, as they swept slowly over the audience, there was also something sad and very vulnerable about those eyes. It seemed to me that this glamorous stage performer was simply acting out a role that had been thrust upon her—a role completely at variance with her nature.

This odd perception passed in a moment. I watched fascinated as Daphne romped about the stage, making rapid-fire predictions and outrageous jokes until she had captured the rapt attention of the audience. Then she was flouncing down a few stairs and onto a narrow walkway, stopping at random first with one member of the audience, then with another, rapidly delivering personal insights, messages from the dead, cosmic advice. There were gasps of disbelief, surprise, embarrassment. "How could she possibly know that?" was typical of the phrases whispered over and over again as Daphne worked her way through the fascinated audience.

I made an appointment with her for a few days hence. When the appointed day came, I drove out to her house in the suburbs.

I saw that I'd been right about those eyes. Daphne's eyes reflected an entirely different persona from that of the dashing blonde I'd seen perform the week before. Her eyes gave the appearance of sadness and vulnerability because, seen at close range, they seemed to be focusing on two realities at once.

I didn't have to suggest this; Daphne soon volunteered that, as she went about her daily life, she was constantly picking up messages and receiving visions, insights and voices from a source other than her five senses. She didn't know how; she only knew she had been experiencing this odd duality of sensation ever since early childhood.

Daphne had been born in Kent, in England, and, after finishing school, she had pursued a career in accounting. She had married and had three children; during all this time she paid little attention to her unusual gift. A series of traumatic changes in her life so deeply intensified her odd sensitivity that she felt she must finally give it free rein. These changes were the death of her adored mother, Daphne's own bitter divorce, and the sudden departure "from the nest" of her own three children now grown. Nothing in her life would be the same again.

Somehow, out of this sorrow and loneliness, there emerged in Daphne an acceptance, an understanding, and a heightened clairvoyance. Soon she decided to give up her career in accounting and spend the rest of her life using her gift to help others. "I realized," she explained to me, "that the energy of love is the only real energy there is."

I asked her if she believed—as I do—that it was the energy of love that had caused the "Big Bang."

"Yes, of course," she replied. "Call it God, call it energy, call it what you will—love causes, permeates, creates, all that is real."

She went on, "What I possess is a gift from God which I must use for the benefit of others. All my predictions, all my clairaudience, all the instructions and admonitions I pass on, are to that end. I do not work like other mediums, and I don't like the word 'channeling.' I am a conduit of the energy of love, not the channel for some disembodied spirit."

Her eyes gazed off into the distance; it was as if her pupils were contracting from some inner light. "I am going to die in a few years," she told me quietly. "It's all right, though. You see, I have a fatal form of cancer, and during my last operation I had a near-death experience that was indescribably beautiful. No one need ever fear death. If one believes in heaven and hell, it is this life on earth which is hell; death delivers you to tranquillity.

"Alas, we're in for some bad times on earth," she told me, sighing deeply. "There will be violent weather changes, surprise catastrophes. If you ask me how we can prepare ourselves for this, I say, 'Love your fellow man, love your neighbor.' It is as simple as that." Daphne's eyes widened and a bright smile spread across her engaging features. "Remember always," she told me with finality, "that the important thing, the thing that will heal the world—is love."

How was Daphne able to 'see' the tube crash? How had she 'known' that a Pan Am plane would be bombed, or that war would break out in the Persian Gulf? Why aren't our brightest scientific minds at least curious about such feats? Perhaps, if such demonstrations of the paranormal as Daphne had exhibited were to be labeled "pathological," the medical world would finally take notice; they could call it the "sixth sense syndrome," and a study of this "syndrome" could be carried out using medical insurance funds or a public health grant.

There must, somehow, be a way to attract serious attention to this crucially important phenomenon.

Chapter 20

Dr. Jean Houston and the Time Compression Effect

As a portrait painter, I have experimented a great deal with light. Throw light on a human face from a particular direction, and that face will appear handsome; redirect the light onto those same features, and they will be rendered less appealing. There are instances where a change of lighting can cause a face to become almost unrecognizable as that seen a moment before. In this case, which is the "real" face? The features haven't altered one centimeter.

Perhaps a psychic is simply someone who can cast light on a person from a different angle.

More fascinating still with respect to lighting is its affect on our perception of time. If we dine under a strong overhead light, for example, we sense the passage of time differently than when we dine by candlelight; it seems that the stronger the light, the more slowly time appears to pass. When the police question a suspect, they place a bright light directly above the suspect's head so that time will seem to drag. Certainly, every hostess knows that if she wants her guests to leave early, she can help implement this by merely increasing the wattage.

I'm never able to ruminate on the subject of the perception of time without thinking of eminent author/psychologist Dr. Jean Houston. Dr. Houston's experiments with time distortion have for years been attracting worldwide attention. She has demonstrated most convincingly that, in an altered state of consciousness, the mind has the capability of compressing time. In one frequently cited experiment—which she describes in her book *The Possible Human*—Dr. Houston demonstrated that, in only a moment of clock time, someone in an altered state of consciousness can 'experience' an hour of piano practice. The result was one hour's worth of improvement in proficiency without a keyboard's ever being touched.

101

Moreover, the fingers and arms were just as tired as they would have been after an hour of intense rehearsal!

Dr. Houston professed no psychic talent herself in the usual sense of the word; but she was certainly so intellectually endowed and so spiritually elevated as to manifest her own unique brand of paranormal giftedness. I wanted very badly to talk with her, so I asked a resourceful friend of mine who knew her well if she would kindly put us in touch. This was not an easy request to fill. Jean Houston's schedule was formidably packed. What with writing books and articles, conducting workshops, travelling on far-flung lecture tours and conducting behavioral experiments, she seemed to have a surefire method of expanding her *own* time.

My friend was finally able to help me reach Dr. Houston by telephone in upstate New York. It was on a Thursday morning, shortly after the globe-trotting psychologist had come back from a seminar in Europe.

From her first enthusiastic, "Hello, Virginia!" I felt that all-embracing empathy which certain rare human beings seem able to extend to all other humans. Dr. Houston readily admitted to me, "*Psi* exists!" I saw I would get no argument from the respected scientist in this regard. But Dr. Houston felt that psychic ability should be regarded as no more than the by-product of a certain development of the intellect and a certain elevation of the spirit—not as an end in itself. In her most recent books *The Possible Human* and *God Seed*, the researcher had sought to guide the reader toward the accomplishment of these twin goals.

As we talked, I again thought of the clairvoyance that was so often attributed to the saints of the Roman Catholic Church. But this clairvoyance, along with manifestations of luminosity, of inedia (the capability of living without food), and even of the stigmata of Christ, were considered by the Church to be merely incidental by-products of the spirituality of these saints, and in no way proof of their sainthood.

Jean Houston talked with me about the power of women to effect change; she spoke of tribal groups living in stress-free societies in the mountains of Ecuador; she talked of metaphysical healing and the patterns that connect—in short, she touched upon a myriad of wide-ranging subjects in a mere and extremely exciting forty-five minutes.

(At least, the clock on the wall said forty-five minutes; with Jean Houston in control, who could be sure?)

In the end, we are forced to wonder if time itself is an illusion. There are those who say that we have simply created time as a convenient tool with which to order events, and that, in reality, everything exists at once! As the revered Far Eastern seer Jagdish Parikh has contended, "All knowledge is already present, and the most we can do is create conditions in which intuition will occur."

Chapter 21

London, England: A Healing
Unique in Medical Annals

Weeks had passed, and I could stand it no longer. I had to call up Gwennie in the hope that by now she had talked to that "young man," as I still thought of him, upon whom she had wrought the most remarkable and unique of all her healings.

Gwennie answered after a number of rings. "Yes, my dear," she told me, "I've talked to Barrie, and he was interested to hear that you think his case might help others."

I learned that his name was Barrie Stonehill and that he was now in his late fifties. Barrie had been born into a prosperous wine-producing family, but, from an early age, he had shown little interest in the purely mundane. He had been a considerate child, always eager to help others. Constantly dependent from his youth on purgatives to relieve his chronic constipation, he had very early on been forced to become conscious of his health—especially when, at the age of 22, his colon had simply ceased to function, and biweekly irrigations had become essential.

Gwennie gave me Barrie's phone number and told me the hours when he was most likely to be reached. I got him on the first try. Barrie's voice was strong and reassuring. He would "of course" be willing to let me write about his cure—or his "change," as he preferred to call it—if somehow this could be of help to others.

Over the phone, we discussed ways in which such a system of elimination through the urine alone could be immensely useful. We discussed at length the potential of such a system for helping colon cancer victims. Even astronauts, whose urine can be treated and recycled, are constantly faced with the problem of the disposal of feces; they have to adhere to very restricted diets to minimize this problem.

"Hasn't anyone ever tried to understand your unusual condition?" I asked.

"I think the medical profession would prefer to simply ignore it," he replied, laughing gently. "It seems to be more of an embarrassment to them than a challenge. Certainly, no one has ever been interested enough to investigate."

"Maybe that's where I come in," I declared, feigning a competence I scarcely felt. How could I, with no credentials save an irrepressible curiosity, be able to convince the medical world that they were overlooking something of startling importance? Here was a phenomenon that was unique, so far as I knew, in the entire annals of the human race!

Our conversation came to an end. In the days to come, I sought out a respected young Atlanta internist, who had not only a brilliant mind, but an open one as well. I drew encouragement from his interest and enthusiasm. He instructed me in the basics of digestion. The more I learned about the human metabolism, the more I was determined to meet with Barrie Stonehill face-to-face. I somehow felt that, to have received Gwennie's spiritual help at all, he must have a remarkable mind himself. I decided I would book a return flight to London for the end of the month.

In the meantime, I made plans to continue my search.

Chapter 22

New York, N.Y.:
A Daughter of the Oracle Solves a Murder Case

There was certainly a "random" element in my encounter with Nancy Baroni, who goes by the *nom de plume* of Joy Herald. I had arrived in New York on a windy March Monday to keep an appointment I'd made a week in advance with quite a different psychic, a woman whose praises I'd heard sung in both Rome and Zagreb. Fame achieved in such widely separated places, I'd decided, must surely be fame deserved.

However, when I arrived at the agreed-upon time at that latter psychic's door, her secretary informed me that all her appointments had been cancelled for the day. This celebrated clairvoyant had been unable to reach me to advise me of the change. Would tomorrow do just as well? I was asked. There would be no way to see her today for sure; it was quite impossible. I was offered no further explanation.

I had only that one day in New York. Feeling discouraged and let down, I put in a telephone call to the American Society for Psychic Research, in search of another clairvoyant. They told me to try the Spiritual Frontiers Fellowship. When I finally got through, I asked if anyone there might know of "someone of interest whom I might interview today—and, yes, it must be today." This would certainly be the very model of the random selection procedure I considered so important!

There was a pause at the end of the line. Then, I was told there was a highly psychic woman living in New Jersey, whom they would telephone on the off chance she might be "coming into the city" on this very day. After a brief wait, they got back to me to tell me that, yes, she would be coming into New York in a very few hours.

This highly psychic woman turned out to be none other than the celebrated Joy Herald. It had only been through a rare set of circumstances that she had been at home and had received the call—

and only through an equally unusual set of circumstances that she had to be in New York that very afternoon. I asked her if she thought this was just a coincidence—or somehow something more? I learned that Joy didn't believe in "coincidences" in the usual sense, but in the synchronicity of Carl Jung.

For the moment, though, our telephone conversation was brief. We agreed on a meeting place. In the short time before I was to see her, I did some quick research, and learned that Joy held two degrees from Catholic University and was sought after as both a lecturer and a radio and TV guest. She had pursued rewarding careers in a number of fields through the years, as a teacher, a publicity director, an insurance broker and an advertising copywriter. Joy was a published poet and an essayist. Add to this her reputation in the field of psychic manifestation, and I hardly knew what to expect.

Certainly, it wasn't the radiant young woman who, blond hair tousled by the wind, came bursting through the door to greet me.

Nothing in Joy Herald's appearance or relaxed demeanor suggested the slightest connection with the occult. She answered my questions directly, without equivocation. It seemed she had received a severe blow to the head as a child, contracted when she fell on the corner of a stone fireplace. That had been the beginning of her voyage into the unknown. From that point on, she said, she'd begun to sense things before they occurred. It hadn't been until she was in college and playing ESP games with her friends that she'd begun to realize the extent of her paranormal gifts.

Later, after her graduation from college, Joy had a psychic experience that opened her eyes to a whole new world. She described this experience as, "a feeling of energy which became more and more intense...there were lights...I heard conversations. It was like being in a time warp. I could feel that the dimensions were many, then feel a fusion of the dimensions." Her clear blue eyes closed briefly as she recalled this moment.

Joy married a young stockbroker, had children, occasionally taught school, and was leading a happy and fulfilled life when she decided it might be interesting to join a group experimenting with mental telepathy. It was then that she found she was adept at what is known as "long distance viewing." She rapidly discovered the range of this unusual gift: "I found I could simply shut my eyes and go into a trance and visions would come totally unbidden. My metabolism would change during these sessions and afterwards I would have a great desire for sweets."

"Are there other physical manifestations?" I asked.

"Yes, an uncomfortable sensation in the back of my head." Joy told me she believed that psychic insights come from the cerebellum, the seat of man's primitive instincts, and that the information she picked up about a client came from the astral projections that surrounded him. "The auric field is so strong that it acts as a transmitter," she explained, adding almost parenthetically an extraordinary fact which I had not been aware of: "Psychics have very long nerve endings—twice as long as is considered normal."

I wasn't surprised to learn Joy's own nerve endings were extremely long. A mere pinprick caused her acute pain; a trip to the dentist was agony. I wondered if these long nerve endings played a role in the ability of religious mystics to manifest the stigmata.

Joy described for me the role she had played in the solving of a tragic murder case—the murder case with which I began this book. This was the series of murders committed by a psychotic serial killer whose last victim was found in a lake in Tallman Park, just as Joy predicted when she 'saw' water and a tall man.

That had not been the end of the investigation for Joy. Having assisted the police in their search for the body, she had gone on to help them track down the killer.

"However did you manage to do this?" I asked her, fascinated.

She explained: "I put myself into a trance. Then, quite suddenly, I 'saw' a man wearing a welding mask. I was told, however, that none of the known suspects worked as a welder.

"But I was so sure of this that I insisted to the police I was certain the man was a welder. Finally, one man among the group being questioned emerged as the prime suspect. Having obtained a warrant to search his house, the police were startled to find in a dark corner of the basement a welding arc and mask!

"It turned out that the suspect's weekend hobby was welding."

Boosted by Joy's vision, the police pressed ahead confidently with their questioning, until the killer—the weekend welder—confessed to the series of depraved crimes.

In a later incident under police investigation, there had been several suspects, any one of whom could have had an opportunity to commit the crime in question. The case was a particularly baffling one, and this time it was the police themselves who sought out Joy for help.

She hadn't been following the case, but she agreed to do whatever she could to aid them in their investigation. It was decided that the detective in charge would write out the names of the possible suspects, place each name in a separate envelope, and give these envelopes to Joy for her "impressions."

Joy told me she'd taken the envelopes one at a time and held them in her hands. "It can't be this one," she began, "nor this one—nor this." Finally, she narrowed the envelopes down to three.

"It's one of these," she told police, "but I can't quite get which one." She put herself into a trance state and allowed the process of automatic writing to take over. Slowly, her hand wrote out four letters. When the envelopes were opened, those letters were the first four letters of the name of one of the suspects. The police focused their questioning on this particular man, who later confessed to the baffling burglary and is now in prison.

How was it that the face of the man in the welding mask had come into Joy's vision while she was concentrating on the serial murder? And why, while she was using automatic writing to attempt to solve the grand larceny case, had Joy's hand suddenly stopped, after writing only the first four letters of the culprit's name? Had she lost the connection with whatever source of universal knowledge she'd been tapping into? What prevented her from "automatically" writing the remaining letters? Was it simply that these four letters were enough?

At one time Joy had worked on a research project at the Psychophysical Laboratory on the Forrestal Campus of Princeton University. She had been observed under laboratory conditions and been found to have powers of perception and insight for which there was no discernable explanation.

I reflected that this had happened back in the 70s, and I wondered: If we were to observe Joy today, with more modern tools, would we end up discovering some answers?

Joy quickly changed the subject. She laughingly recalled a long ago reading that had dramatically changed a client's life. A young unmarried woman, suffering from recurring headaches, had come to her one day for help. Joy had advised the woman to stop the heavy medication she was taking, then discussed with her colors she should introduce into her environment. As the reading continued, Joy 'saw' that the client should wear an amethyst. "You should buy a piece of jewelry containing amethyst; that is your gem," she told the woman.

The client stopped taking her medication. The headaches went away. Perhaps on account of the effectiveness of Joy's advice, the client went shopping for an amethyst. Making the rounds of a large jewelry store, she came upon a beautiful amethyst ring. She asked the handsome young man behind the counter if she could try it on. She bought the ring that afternoon, and a few months later married that same young man.

Joy told me that for some time she had been conducting an unusual sort of lost and found service throughout the U.S.: She used her psychic power to locate lost persons, lost animals and lost or stolen jewelry. She explained that when she tuned in on a loss, the third finger of her right hand became very hot. She then took a large regional map and let her finger pass over it till the digit was drawn down to a particular spot on the map; the search was now narrowed down to a particular area. Joy would then make a detailed map of the targeted area and let her finger continue the search.

I asked her if she had actually located missing persons. "Oh, yes," she replied quickly. "But sometimes with very sad results. Recently, two business executives taking a flight in a company plane literally disappeared. I was given a map of the general territory over which they were traveling. I suddenly experienced something like a gust of wind, and felt as if my finger was being pushed down onto a certain spot on the map. The authorities carefully searched the area indicated by my finger and, in the heavy underbrush, they found the plane. There was every evidence that the crash had been caused by a strong downdraft."

Joy's method had many applications. Recently, she had received a request to "psychometrize" an area in Africa in an attempt to find out where elephants were being poached. She told me she was able to use the same method to locate oil, or water—or even gold. She speculated that oil companies would be able to make routine use of such techniques in the future. "Genuine psychics have been found to have an accuracy record equaling that of seismographic instruments," she added. "They are certainly less expensive!"

Recalling that distance was not a factor in psychic seeing, I remarked to Joy, "Shouldn't our government be using clairvoyants in dealing with other nations?"

"Well, if not," she replied, "they are certainly failing to exploit a resource that could potentially provide nations with protection."

There was so much I wanted to ask her. Were psychics ever used in cases where we were unsure of a person's identity? What about the woman who claimed to be Anastasia, sole surviving member of the Russian royal family? Or the man thought to be Joseph Mengele, the sadistic surgeon of the Nazi concentration camps?

"I don't know about that," Joy answered, "but I do know that psychics are being made use of in the art world, because recently I was approached about a matter involving a great deal of money and the dubious origins of a particular work of art."

We talked long into the afternoon. Joy recounted many personal experiences of insight and synchronicity. Despite her busy schedule, which included counseling, past life regression and healing, she was now writing a book on the multidimensionality of the universe.

Before I left, Joy let me glance through a large stack of newspaper clippings about her work. One in particular caught my eye, a

New Jersey headline that read: **"PSYCHIC 'SAW' MASSACHU-SETTS AIR CRASH."** The article quoted witnesses who testified to Joy's helping them find the lost company plane I earlier referred to. The story read:

"The third finger of psychic Nancy Baroni (Joy Herald) zeroed in on the general location of the wreck of a twin engine Cessna 310 on a map two weeks before the downed aircraft was discovered."

The article reported that other psychics had been used to search for the missing plane, but that none of them had provided clues as specific as Joy's.

I put the clippings back in the neat stack and looked at Joy in wonderment. Her smile, her warmth, her relaxed and easy charm—these made me almost forget that Joy possessed an awesome gift: the capability of seeing beyond the confines of accepted reality.

Chapter 23

Washington, D.C.: "Everything Goes On and On, and God Is in Control"

Though Maude Chalfant hailed from a small Southwestern town, she now made her home in Washington, D.C. One afternoon, I followed the directions she'd carefully given me and arrived at the door of her flat in a large building near the center of the nation's capital.

Entering through a narrow hallway, I found myself in a bright, spacious room cluttered with a wide assortment of rare and lovely art objects. So unusual were they, and so unrelated in their variety, that they gave no consistent clue as to their owner's interests. I trod gingerly through this intriguing maze of treasures which seemed to overflow the tables, the chests, the cabinets and the bookshelves. "Over here, over here!" A warm, urgent voice directed me toward the satin-covered sofa at the far end of the room. Maude Chalfant turned out to be a tall gracious woman with beautiful features, from whom there positively radiated what I could only call an unconditional love of humanity. I'd heard extravagant praise of her psychic powers; but no one had prepared me for the sheer joy and goodness that seemed to emanate from deep within her.

Maude also had a certain innate reticence, which she finally agreed to set aside so she could tell me about herself. She hadn't always been so happy, she said. As a child, she'd been rather large for her age; and, despite an I.Q. which tested in the genius range and a precocious gift for the piano, she had been ill-at-ease and awkward among her peers.

At about age six, she suffered a severe head injury; shortly afterward, she'd begun to experience what is known as astral traveling. The frightened child saw herself leaving her body and floating over the heads of the people around her. Whenever the phone rang, she immediately knew who was calling. She found she could even envision events before they happened.

Her early school days were miserable. Maude felt isolated, as if she didn't belong. Not only was she taller than her classmates, but she experienced odd sensations she could neither deny nor explain. I reminded her of Carl Jung's words: "If a man knows more than others, he becomes quite lonely."

As we were speaking I thought of the words of psychiatrist Dr. Lee Sannella, who once said, "Child psychics may have it difficult from the start, because of the disturbing and disruptive nature of their genius."

During her college years, Maude had a particularly memorable astral projection; she described it for me in a quiet voice, her eyes focused faraway. "One quiet evening, I was watching the twinkling stars and feeling the wind. Suddenly, I looked up at the sky, and noticed a particularly brilliant star. In the next moment, I was on that star! I heard a voice saying, 'You must not worry. Everything goes on and on, and God is in control.'"

Maude never forgot those words or that particular phraseology—which, one day, she would hear again, under very different circumstances.

After college she moved to Washington and took a job in a large government office, glad to be away from the small town mentality she'd found so stifling as a child.

Maude was curious about the strange insights that still randomly possessed her. She accompanied a friend to a seance, and, to her surprise, while she was there she abruptly slipped into a deep trance lasting several hours. From that evening on, her psychic powers blossomed with ever-increasing rapidity, so much so that her family became frightened for her.

One day, Maude found herself able to demonstrate automatic writing. During one of these sessions, she predicted the date of the end of World War II in Europe—a date which proved to be completely accurate. Given her musical talent and training, it was a little less surprising that in the trance state she began to channel the voices and the piano techniques of a series of long-dead musicians. Once, while in trance, she threw back her head and began to sing in a voice remarkably like that of Swedish singer Jenny

114

Lind. "The music guides never fail me," Maude stated with conviction.

I'd noticed several skillfully executed pastel and charcoal drawings and hadn't imagined they were Maude's own works until she told me that painters and sculptors "came through" her as well. She explained that while she was in trance she was able to create works of art never possible for her while she was in her normal state.

When we discussed Maude's ability to predict psychically, she looked pensively off into the distance. "It is all a circle," she said, speaking softly, "and sometimes, sometimes, we can see across it."

When giving readings, Maude had never received messages directly portending death, but she had sometimes been told enough to give a warning. "I very seldom go into a trance when giving readings," she told me, "and I'm always completely frank. I don't just tell people what they want to hear.

"Twenty years ago, I saw what was taking place in the world today, but I was told by my spirit guides that I should not grieve, that there was a plan for everything." Maude's eyes had brightened as, with quiet confidence, she stated this. "What we are getting today is only a tiny glimpse."

Maude confessed she had always felt a "strong sense of God." She was very active in her Washington church, where she gave what she referred to as "psychic concerts;" she meant her channeled singing. These concerts led to an unusual incident. A young minister, who particularly liked the concerts, showed his appreciation by bringing Maude a beautiful necklace from New Mexico. When he gave her the necklace, he told Maude that the old Indian from whom he'd bought it had spoken the following enigmatic words: "Take this to the one to whom it belongs. Everything goes on and on."

These words were the same Maude had heard on the star.

Maude Chalfant seemed to me to be a fulfilled and contented person. She had a wide circle of friends and had attracted people into her life who were, as she put it, "in sympathy." She felt very humble when she reflected on the awesome powers she was able to demonstrate. "It's all God," she told me simply. "It's all God!"

Chapter 24

Dr. Andrija Puharich Tests a Renowned Psychic as She Journeys to the Planet Ogatta

"I believe I know why the ESP experiments at Duke University haven't achieved greater results. You know, the ones with the flash cards, where the sender on one side of a wall concentrates on a given card and tries mentally to send a picture of the card to a receiver on the other side of the wall. The rate of success is low because there's no emotional content. Why not have an elderly Jew concentrate on a card bearing a swastika? Or a failed priest concentrate on a card bearing a cross?"

This conversation took place with a friend as we drove through the Georgia countryside on our way to North Carolina to meet Greta Woodrew, a woman whose powers of extrasensory perception were recognized worldwide.

Tall, handsome Greta Woodrew was a veritable dynamo of energy as she bounded down the circular staircase in her spacious mountain home to greet us. She laughed, she talked, she shook our hands—she enveloped us in her vast warmth and enthusiasm. Greta's ebullient vitality electrified the entire room, and made the rest of us look by comparison wilted and enervated after our long journey.

There was so much to tell! She was so eager to begin!

If I hadn't read Greta's books, I would never have been able to anticipate what I was about to hear: Her extrasensory experiences had opened up whole new possibilities for the human mind. Greta Woodrew's story led me to the inevitable conclusion that the human brain can receive messages from intelligent life in other parts of the universe.

Who was this remarkable Greta Woodrew anyway? Her curriculum vitae read like an entry in a *Who's Who* of America's most successful career women. She held two degrees; she had served as president of an executive search firm and vice-president of a large chain of department stores; she had four children who were now grown; and she had a delightful husband.

In such a full and happy life, the presence of ESP must almost have seemed an intrusion; and so it had first seemed to Greta. When, as a child, she initially became aware of her psychic abilities, she had tried to ignore them, profiting instead from her rapidly-maturing intellectual abilities to excel in her studies and prepare herself for what would be a highly successful career. By so doing, however, she had unwittingly acquired the very credentials which would make it difficult for the normally discerning person to dismiss her paranormal experiences. How could anyone so wonderfully competent in the world be "crazy," or even "weird?"

In December, 1976, Greta had agreed to participate in a research project carried out in the U.S. by famed Brazilian medical doctor and researcher Andrija Puharich. Dr. Puharich had set up his own laboratory for the investigation of the physiochemical basis of paranormal phenomena. He, too, had impeccable credentials; the distinguished medical researcher, who died in 1995, held numerous patents in medicine and electronics, some of them contributing to the development of the hearing aid. Dr. Puharich had also written a number of successful and controversial books, including *Uri* (on Uri Geller), *The Sacred Mushroom* and *Beyond Telepathy*.

At the beginning of each session, Dr. Puharich placed Greta in a hypnotic state. Greta described for me the sensations she remembered feeling at the time. She had felt as if she were floating, as if part of herself had left her body; her sense of time had disappeared. She had been about to astrally project herself when suddenly she saw "a man who was wearing silver all over, like a costume...a birdlike creature. Then there was a long dark tunnel, and a manlike creature standing there with a birdlike face and human eyes—marvelous eyes, golden, human eyes." Greta recalled that she'd begun to speak in a very low voice. When her words were played back to her afterward, she insisted this was "the first time I have heard such a voice come through me. I couldn't possibly consciously make a sound like that through my body."

So that neither audio nor electrical frequencies could penetrate into his lab and interfere with the experiments, Dr. Puharich had constructed a room encased entirely in copper. It was into this room that Greta was conducted for the next session. Again, she heard voices; again, there was the long dark tunnel.

During the third session, Greta was able to make her way completely through the tunnel. She found herself in a place where she felt completely known. Smiling faces, and tiny arms reaching up to her, made her feel infinitely welcomed and loved. The beings gave her a name: Plura. Greta was filled with an immense joy; she felt she had come home. And her home was a planet named Ogatta.

The experience was enormously unsettling to her, but not because of its strangeness. On the contrary: The out-of-body experience in Dr. Puharich's laboratory had reawakened in her a long-forgotten memory of a strange event that had taken place when she was only three-and-a-half, and had been taken to New York to visit her grandmother. She had heard a voice, and then, out of nowhere, someone had seemed to appear before her. Greta remembered that she was neither startled nor frightened by this initial visit—even though she realized that the visitor was not human.

Greta recalled the being's saying, "I'm going to take you out to where the others await you."

The episode had not been merely the escape from reality of a lonely little girl. Greta had had a happy childhood; she had been surrounded by wonderful parents and adoring relatives and friends. But she found that when she told them about her strange experiences—beginning with this encounter with the little being—they tended to ascribe them simply to her vivid imagination.

One person, however, understood: her beloved uncle, the family patriarch, who had psychic abilities himself. Without the confidence her uncle instilled in her, she told me, she might even have dismissed the visions herself.

Greta Woodrew's "cosmic adventures" went on for six years after this initial encounter at her grandmother's. She had indeed been taken, "out there." "Out there," she explained to me, was a place far from the earth, clean and beautiful, filled with flowers and permeated by a marvelous scent. There was music you could see, colors you could hear, and the inhabitants, called the Ogattans, had a mission: to help us on earth to build a better future.

These long-buried memories came flooding back to Greta when, many years later, she was greeted by the Ogattans in the copper-encased chamber of Dr. Puharich's laboratory. She described the various members of the Ogattan group to me. She told me how the visits had gone on and on, and how these wonderful beings still appeared to her at random, telling her again and again that she had been chosen by the Ogattans to carry their message to earth.

"Would you like to see something interesting?" Greta asked me suddenly. "Close your eyes and hold out your hand. Do you feel anything?" When I opened my eyes, there lay in the palm of my hand a white, fluffy, virtually weightless tuft of—

"That's a feather of the *kitzber* bird, one of the loveliest of all the Ogattan birds," said Greta. "These birds resemble our doves, but they experience our atmosphere as being extremely heavy."

"How on earth did you get it?" I exclaimed, too startled to notice that I'd made an obvious pun. Laughing, Greta proceeded with the following account:

It had transpired that an Ogattan named Tauri, speaking through Greta, had once asked Dr. Puharich and Greta's son, Alan, if they would like to have a feather from the *kitzber* bird. Both nodded, not knowing what to expect. Greta asked them to get empty envelopes and put them in their laps. They complied. Greta asked them to look inside the envelopes. Each was amazed to find a white, fluffy, tuft-like object: the feather of the *kitzber* bird!

Greta told me that these feathers, when subjected to analysis, proved to be of no known origin. The one she'd placed in my hand had belonged to Alan.

It was not hard to understand that these visits from the Ogattans would have significantly changed the direction of Greta's life. To her own convictions about what she had seen and heard, she was able to add the documented findings of Dr. Andrija Puharich who, after he had tested her in his laboratory, had declared Greta to be "one of the leading psychics in the world today, or in any day."

It had seemed mandatory, then, that she give the fullest attention to her powers.

Greta and her highly intelligent and supportive husband determined to pool their considerable resources, leave their Connecticut home, and buy a mountaintop in North Carolina.

There they established the Space, Technology and Research Foundation, where they now devoted their time and money not only to the investigation of ESP and psychic healing, but also to helping the human race prepare for what lay in store.

"Planet Earth is destined for changes on a grand scale," Greta predicted, her voice becoming very earnest. "These changes will not occur overnight; they are happening gradually." Finally: "Those best-prepared for the changes will make the smoothest transition."

Since she was exhibiting tireless vitality throughout the entire afternoon, it was not surprising that Greta often spoke of energy. "All of the universe is energy," she declared exuberantly to me, "creative energy, transforming energy, annihilating energy! It is the life force, the life-continuum."

Greta had understood the uses of this energy so well that she could bend spoons and move objects. Glass cases placed here and there throughout the house contained the silverware (now twisted into odd shapes) that had yielded to her telekinetic powers.

"How, Greta, how?" I asked her, pointing to a very distorted salad fork.

She showed me a passage in her book, *Memories of Tomorrow*, in which she had written, "You do it by removing the pattern by which it has been set. You are unwinding the field that binds its atoms into those patterns. You are allowing it to bend to the pattern you have envisioned in your mind. Gently, you remove the energies that hold it in its present form, and allow the atoms the freedom to move into the pattern that you present. Just as you can talk to plants, you can talk to spoons as well, with love as the greatest positive energy of all. Love the spoon and allow it to bend."

Due to these quite visible demonstrations of her unusual power and understanding, Greta was in demand at conferences all over the world. Hers was a message of hope; she was convinced that human nature was changing for the better. "A higher form of humanity is beginning to emerge on our planet," she assured me.

Greta maintained that the focal point of extrasensory perception was the solar plexus, "that area from the top of the diaphragm to just below the navel; it ties in a whole network of nerves from the automatic nervous system. With training and constant practice, we can all learn to be psychic. It's really an ancient ability which we have buried. All living things pulsate, radiate; the aborigines have communicated telepathically for 40,000 years. We've simply allowed the gift to grow dormant within ourselves.

"This applies to healing as well," she pursued. "Everyone is capable of tapping into the earth's energy to heal themselves and others. Healing is the restoration of balance. Remember, the power of the mind is awesome. You can make yourself sick by approaching a situation with a negative attitude. All mental aberration—guilt, disappointment, repressed emotion—affect the body; if they are not addressed, illness will result. The healer and the one being healed work together. We are all instigating our own miracles. We must not totally relegate the responsibility of our bodies to anyone else."

Healing now occupied a large part of her time. Greta explained that she used her thoughts to literally focus the life force of energy onto the person being healed. "With practice, we can all learn to focus this energy," she declared, "but it takes practice, practice, practice."

Greta constantly assured all her patients that it was they themselves who were responsible for their own healing, and that it was their trust that enabled them to receive the force of healing energy. This in turn enabled the mind to achieve cell-to-cell communication within the body; as a result, harmony and balance were re-established.

Greta's husband worked closely with her at these healing sessions, and was in complete accord with her ideas. The two told me about the recent healing of a 62-year-old man, whose pancreatic cancer had left him with a life expectancy of no more than three months. After only thirteen days, he had been able to leave the mountaintop completely cured.

I wasn't surprised to learn that Greta had been a friend of the late Helen Keller, whom she described as, "a magnificent example of the ability to pick up normal communication in an extrasensory way." Greta recalled the afternoon when she had taken one of her young daughters to call on Miss Keller, who, deaf, dumb and blind since infancy, had overcome these deficiencies and even become a figure of world-renown. "What beautiful red hair," Miss Keller had exclaimed, "and what a beautiful blue dress."

"How can she tell?" the child had whispered to her mother.

"You don't have to whisper," Greta had told her. "She can't hear."

How indeed had Helen Keller known? Greta explained it in this way: "Perhaps all colors have frequencies, and when the usual receiver is broken, another way will be found to pick up those frequencies. Helen Keller had learned to pick up color frequencies through her hands. We should realize that our senses needn't be impaired for us to pick up information in a paranormal way."

I thought to myself that Helen Keller had never been described as "flaky;" and I wondered again why skepticism always surrounded those otherwise normal people who could perform similar feats.

Before leaving, I asked Greta more about the Ogattans. I learned that they had imparted to her bits of their own strange vocabulary and the meaning of each word. She had published these in her first book, *On a Slide of Light,* inviting anyone who also understood the words to get in touch with her. Literally thousands of letters had poured in, all of them with the wrong answers—except for two, one from a schoolboy in California, and the other from a woman in China.

In both cases, Greta had immediately gotten on a plane and flown to meet the person, thinking, "Thank God, I'm validated; the Ogattans are real!" Her eyes filled with tears when she told me of her meetings with these two people so significant in her life.

From her mountaintop retreat, Greta was sending out messages of hope. Not the least of these was that our mind is a vastly unexplored world, and that the future is an endlessly exciting one.

But Greta did envision troubled times just ahead. She felt that the Ogattans were dedicated to helping us weather them. She believed that extra-terrestrial stimuli now impinging upon our planet made it easier for people with inherent extrasensory abilities to develop those gifts. "We shall need these sensitives—their awarenesses beyond the five senses—in the trying times ahead," she quietly added.

While we were driving home, I thought long and hard about Greta Woodrew and her extra-terrestrial friends. J.B. Priestly had once written that the universe must contain "innumerable levels of being of which we are ignorant."

I thought anew of Christ's words, "I have other worlds."

In discussing her healing work, Greta had mentioned the name of Virginia Rich Barrett, the celebrated ballerina who was the associate director of the Carl Radcliffe Dance Group and—though she was in her late fifties—still one of the principal performers with the Atlanta-based group. It occurred to me that here was someone who might be able to give me a first-hand account of what went on during one of Greta Woodrew's psychic healings. I decided to call her, and for that reason I was all the more eager to get back to Atlanta.

Our meeting took place a few days later. Virginia Barrett, vibrant and sparkling—looking half her age—met me at the door when I arrived to talk about Greta. Her first words were, "Come in, come in! Nothing would please me more than to tell you how this wonderful woman saved my career."

Some two years before she'd met Greta, Virginia's right knee had become so stiff and swollen that she could hardly make it back to her dressing room after each performance. Forced at length to give up dancing completely, she had decided to submit to exploratory surgery to discover the source of the problem.

In the course of the procedure, the doctors discovered that all the cartilage on either side of her kneecap was badly torn—so much so that pieces of cartilage had worked their way into the knee joints. Virginia was forced to confront a terrible prognosis: Not only would she never be able to dance again, but she would never be able to participate in any form of callisthenics or sports again. For someone whose career—whose entire life—was dependent upon using her body effectively, such news was totally devastating. This was a death sentence.

Virginia had to remain in bed for several days while recovering from the surgery. During this time, she happened to read a book by Greta Woodrew in which healing was discussed. Virginia picked up the phone in desperation and called Greta, a perfect stranger, to ask if she might come to her for help. Greta immediately assented.

"What happened when you got there?" I eagerly asked.

"You've seen Greta's beautiful place in the mountains? Upstairs, in the north wing, she has a small sunny room which she calls her 'healing room.' Greta and her husband had to literally carry me up the stairs to that room. Because of the recent surgery, my knee was more swollen than ever; every movement caused me excruciating pain.

"Greta bade me lie down on a couch and stated calmly, 'Now, either one of three things will happen. You'll be healed immediately. Or there will be some improvement, and your knee will continue to improve. Or there will be no change at all. I can never tell beforehand which one of these will take place.' She sat down facing me. Her husband stood behind her, hands planted firmly on her shoulders, 'to keep me grounded,' Greta explained briefly. Then she went into an altered state of consciousness."

"You mean into a trance state?" I asked.

"I guess that's what some people would call it. In any event, she closed her eyes after telling me I could keep mine open or closed, it didn't matter.

"Then she took a deep breath and put her hands very gently on my leg; she barely touched it. She moved her hands very slowly up and down my leg, up and down my leg. Whenever her hands brushed the swollen skin around my knee, there was a sensation of velvety softness.

"Suddenly, she made a swift pass under my knee, then held out her hand. 'Look!' she exclaimed. In the bottom of her hand lay a pool of mucus. The odor was dreadful! 'Toxic material,' Greta quietly explained. I looked down at my knee. To my amazement, I couldn't see an opening anywhere through which the mucus could have escaped—though possibly it could have escaped through some sort of osmosis, I suppose. In five minutes all the swelling had gone down, and the knee looked perfectly normal. I could even go up and down Greta's stairs now—which, believe me, I did over and over again on that wonderful afternoon. Here it was, only five days after surgery, and the pain was completely gone.

"Greta assured me, 'You have no more disease in that knee.' She also cautioned me that, 'Like any athlete who hasn't been able to practice, you're out of condition. You must take it slowly as you build back to your normal proficiency.'

"Two months later, I was back on stage! My surgeon—who had told me she would have to see it to believe it—was in the audience with my husband on that memorable night. As she watched me execute a particularly demanding maneuver, she turned to him and humbly said:

"'There is so much we don't understand.'"

Chapter 25

London, England: Summit Meeting of Healer, Healed, Reporter, and Cat

I read an article once that made me wonder if the rejection of all claims to *psi* phenomena by scientists might not simply be a sub-conscious attempt on their part to protect themselves physically. The article stated that in the bodies of those forced to abandon long-held belief systems, the sodium level dropped markedly relative to the potassium level. Almost immediately, they became completely exhausted. "This is how the adrenaline glands react to a loss of face," I'd thought smugly to myself.

But now I had to remind myself that there were certain exceptions among scientists—like the internist I'd talked to about Barrie. The possibility of *psi* didn't seem to affect the sodium level of this brilliant young doctor; he'd only become more and more interested as I told him about Gwennie's cure. He wasn't threatened. There was still hope in the medical establishment.

I couldn't wait to get home and start packing for my trip to England, where I would meet Gwennie's Barrie Stonehill at last.

Once I arrived in London, it didn't take long for me to find my way back to Gwennie Scott's living room. This was where the three of us had agreed to meet. I felt as if somehow I were treading on hallowed ground, as if these two knew things they could never tell me because I could never understand. I should add that the ginger-colored cat was also present at this meeting, stealing quietly in to join us. "She's deaf," Gwennie had said, holding her close. "That's why she never meows, poor thing. She's never heard a 'meow' in all her life, and so she never gives one."

I'm not sure what I'd been expecting, but I found Barrie's physical appearance something of a surprise. He was tall, lean, and ruggedly handsome, with a steady gaze in his quiet blue eyes. His words were measured, his voice firm, as he answered the many questions I put to him.

Barrie first of all told me that, without really thinking about it, he had given up using doctors after the change in his digestive system, becoming—and this was hardly a surprise—intensely interested in psychic surgery and spiritual healing in general.

This had led to more than one remarkable encounter. Barrie told me he'd once taken a friend with failing eyesight to the renowned healer Odelon, in Brazil. Odelon had called various people up from the audience. Barrie watched in awe as, with a word here, a gesture there, the Brazilian healer seemed to cure them all. The audience stared in amazement as tumors apparently dissolved with a simple manipulation of the healer's fingers. A small cross-eyed boy was summoned to the platform. Odelon touched the back of the boy's head, and the eyes uncrossed immediately! The child left the platform with completely normal vision.

Odelon stopped abruptly. His eyes slowly scanned the audience. He looked directly at Barrie, and commanded him to come up on the platform. Barrie complied. The famous Odelon pointed at Barrie's abdomen and shouted: "What is this? What healer has done this? This is the most remarkable man in the world! Everything he eats goes into another dimension. He doesn't use his colon at all!"

"How do *you* explain all this?" I asked Barrie in amazement.

Barrie shook his head. "I don't know. It must be a strong mental energy."

We turned to Gwennie for help.

"Well, Barrie," she said, "as you know, I had to go into trance for your healing. It's hard to explain, but it was as though different vibrations were coming through and looking at your problem." Gwennie spoke very slowly. "They said they wanted to experiment. In the end, they actually changed your metabolism."

"'They?' Who are 'they'?" I asked.

Gwennie's eyes half-closed, as if she were reliving those moments. "The spirit guides were a Dr. Karl Lubrecht, who lived in the late 1800s, and a Dr. Oppenheim and Dr. Lso Wong, who'd lived hundreds of years earlier. I remember asking Dr. Lso Wong, 'What does your name mean?' and the answer he gave me was, 'It means nothing, because I am not really Chinese.' He claimed he had merged with another personality."

I wondered if while she was in trance Gwennie's subconscious mind, sensing what was taking place in Barrie's body, had invented the three doctors and their experiment to explain what was happening, just as we invent explanations while in the dream state for physical sensations we experience while asleep. When a child has kicked his covers off at night and lies shivering in bed, he may well be dreaming he's in a snowstorm; his subconscious has created the dream to explain his physical sensations.

Barrie continued with his account. "Not long after my amazing change, I visited a well-known medium. My family doctor, Dr. Louis Shear, who'd recently died, came through and told me, 'You've been given special powers to deal with your problem. Do you remember those injections I was giving you before I died? I want you to stop them immediately. You no longer need them.'"

Barrie confessed that from that moment he had begun to seek out people who claimed to have extraordinary powers. He became disenchanted with many of them, but he had also found many whose claims were valid. He described the famed Indian swami Dev Murti, said to have trained his automatic nervous system from early childhood to do anything he commanded. "He would take unused lengths of railroad track for his demonstrations," Barrie told us. "He was able to wind the heavy rails around his little finger. Though he was small of stature, he could hold an airplane down on the ground while it was accelerating. He would allow steamrollers to run over his body while he was lying on a bed of glass."

Gwennie merely shrugged, obviously unimpressed. She declared that, "Once, I psyched myself up and thrust a large knitting needle through my arm, with no bleeding or pain whatsoever. There is a state of mind where you are completely in control, where you can become completely detached." Gwennie was all set to dismiss the subject entirely.

Exactly what was involved in Greta's psyching-up process? I wondered. Not many months before, I had watched a group of

Hindu devotees dancing through the streets of Singapore with metal skewers stuck through their cheeks and tongues. They were celebrants of Thaipusan Day; as they danced, they experienced neither pain nor bleeding. Cheered on by friends and family, the group had arrived without mishap at their destination, a colorful Hindu temple in the middle of the city.

I'd watched at close range as the skewers were withdrawn. Not a drop of blood fell, there was no mark on cheek or tongue, to suggest that these body parts of the celebrants had been pierced just a moment before; the skin or the membrane had simply closed up. I learned that this unusual practice of prayer and thanksgiving took place once a year, and that it was preceded by weeks of fasting and rigorous emotional and mental preparation. Had Gwennie subjected herself to such a preparation? Could Jean Houston's time compression hypnosis be used to speed up this preparation period? What possibilities there were here for surgery without anesthesia!

I was anxious to get back into the conversation. "Do you think what happened to Barrie might indicate a new direction in our evolution?" I asked. "Might the colon one day become as obsolete as the appendix?"

Suddenly, Gwennie got up and started toward the entrance to the kitchen. "It's after one," she exclaimed. "You must be starved."

She had prepared a delicious lunch for us. We ate in a small dining room overlooking a garden, graced by Gwennie's two cats blinking lazily in the sunlight. Out of the corner of my eye, I saw that Barrie seemed to relish every morsel of food that was put before him. "I eat everything," he remarked, as if reading my mind. "I eat fibrous meat, vegetables, fruits, cooked or raw—anything and everything. Gwennie's miracle certainly didn't affect my appetite!"

The visit ended on this mundane note of food. I've always heard that the ingestion of proteins tends to bring our thoughts down to earth. Whether this was true or not, our talk of higher dimensions had come to end. We said goodbye and vowed to "keep in touch."

Once returned to Atlanta, I met again with the internist who'd shown such an interest in Barrie's case. This young physician had decided to invite Barrie to America so that his condition could be observed and investigated. In his letter to my friend this internist had written words that I continue to wish every scientist could read:

"If we can discover a way to apply the development in your system to others, the benefits will be tremendous."

Chapter 26

Honolulu, Hawaii: Tarot Cards as Suggestions, not Pronouncements

Early the next day, I departed for the Far East. Even as my plane climbed above the clouds, I found I was still preoccupied with Barrie Stonehill. I wondered if he would actually consider coming to America, if he would actually be willing to let himself be put through tests and sometimes unpleasant exploratory procedures. The answer was that maybe he would; Gwennie had told me many times that there was nothing Barrie liked better than helping others.

I hoped the internist would have received an answer by the time I got back to Atlanta.

My destination was Taiwan's capital, Taipei, but I had made an arrangement for a stopover in Honolulu, Hawaii. It was there I found a young psychic who used Tarot cards to augment her insights. She introduced herself as Karima Tatum.

As it turned out, Karima was not only young but exotically attractive. Her name, when she pronounced it for me, sounded equally exotic, with the stress on the second syllable as in 'ka-RI-ma' and the last syllable trailing off like a wisp of smoke. Karima's gentle smile, her wide dark eyes, her look of total guilelessness, made her appear even younger than her years. She was a musician as well as a psychic, and had been studying music here in Honolulu for several years.

Karima had experienced insights of a psychic nature from a very early age. Over the past 16 years, while pursuing a career in music, she had made an intensive study of the Tarot. Karima's interpretations of the cards went far beyond any specific happenings they might predict. She seemed to be of the school of French occultist Oswald Wirth, who believed there were many different points of view from which the Tarot symbols could be correctly interpreted.

Wirth thought that each thinker would discover unique meanings in the light of his or her own conceptual systems. The occultist believed the symbols were intended merely to evoke ideas and activate thought in a way which would lead inward toward the truth; the ideas and thoughts would necessarily be in accordance with the unique inner nature of the particular person. Wirth had written somewhere that the Tarot symbols helped to put us in touch with our hidden selves.

Karima herself believed the cards were meant only to reveal those qualities within a person which would have some impact on that person's future; the cards were not a reading of the future in itself. She felt predicting specific events could be harmful, warning me that such predictions could become self-fulfilling prophecies. She preferred that our fate be left in our own hands. Karima had decided long ago that the proper use of the Tarot lay in its helping us to know ourselves; it was in this knowing of ourselves, she insisted, that we were able to weed out those destructive habits and emotions which blocked our progress and thwarted us in the realization of our goals. Karima regarded the evocation of such self-knowledge as a form of healing—assuming that the proper diagnosis of an ailment could be said to be the first step toward healing.

"Where do you hope your psychic work will lead?" I asked.

"I hope that I'll get more and more into healing," Karima told me. Her dark brown eyes shone with eagerness in the morning light. "Doing something for others brings the greatest happiness. I urge those for whom I read to listen to their inner voices, to trust their higher instincts. We all have some degree of psychic ability. With the world as it is today, we will surely need it."

Karima now alluded to Carl Jung's belief that unresolved inner conflicts could manifest themselves in a person's outer life.

"Are the links between our thoughts and our fate indeed so definite and traceable?" I asked.

"Certainly," she replied. "Devoid of inner conflicts and the subsequent out-picturing of those conflicts, how different our destinies would be."

Karima went on to stress the importance of never burdening children with a sense of guilt which would make them feel they must somehow contrive to be punished. "We should never cripple children with feelings of inadequacy that can paralyze their chances of success," she told me. "Under the best of circumstances, the instinct for survival is constantly at war with our own self-destructive impulses. The instinct for survival needs all the help it can get."

Karima's final message to me was this: "With the help of the Tarot, I can enable people to know themselves more fully and therefore look critically at the directions their lives are taking. I am afraid I often interpret the symbols differently from other Tarot readers. But, for me, the symbols act only as a catalyst for my own insights."

Chapter 27

Taipei, Taiwan: *Swan Min* and the Artist as Oracle

While I was in flight to Taipei, I pondered Karima's warnings regarding our self-destructive impulses, those foolish acts against ourselves that we often commit. Karima had also reminded me that our self-images were frequently erroneous. In his death-bed message to his son, Iskander of Balph had addressed this subject of self-deception eloquently, saying: "What you imagine to be yourself is concocted from beliefs put into you by others, and is not yourself at all."

I thought back to my first visit to Taiwan, or Formosa as it was then called, and to a troubling tableau that is forever etched in my memory. It vividly illustrated Karima's warnings about our mistaken self-images. The tableau had unfolded almost a generation ago; it had taken place as I was arriving at a fashionable restaurant in the heart of downtown Taipei. I happened to witness a very old woman being carried through the entrance of the restaurant by her two middle-aged sons, their arms crossed sedan-chair fashion in order to support her slender frame. From the tiny satin slippers she wore, I knew that the woman's feet were bound; that they had been bound in infancy so she would never be expected to walk, this being a mark of luxury and privilege. The scene was a sad reminder of a custom which had once been practiced with pride, but which had been based on an image of woman which we now consider to be cruelly misguided. It was the sort of self-imaging that Karima had warned me about, and the best that could be said for it was that it was no longer being practiced, which did suggest a modicum of progress on our part.

I made my way to my destination through a Taipei in which three decades had passed since such scenes could be glimpsed. Behind a wide red-lacquered door on the capital's bustling Chung North Road, there lay a plant-filled courtyard leading to a secluded and pleasant house. It was the home of the clairvoyant Chang Chuen Shang. She lived in this house with her elderly father, a noted calligrapher, who from his daughter's early childhood had been her mentor in the practice of *swan min*.

What is *swan min*? It is clairvoyance, it is fortune-telling—call it what you will, the word translates into the use of the sixth sense.

I was received in an anteroom where two caged Mina birds vyed unceasingly with each other as to who could scream the louder. This caused Chuen Shang obvious discomfort, while her father—admittedly quite deaf—seemed totally unaware of the disturbance. Throughout the interview, the noted calligrapher's face remained as inscrutable as a croupier's at a gambling table.

The Shang family had a gift for prognostication that went back a long way. Chuen Shang's greatgrandfather was so well respected as a prognosticator that the priests consulted him whenever they needed to choose a grave site. The family could trace its lineage back to a prime minister in the Ming Dynasty (1368-1644 A.D.); there were clairvoyants among its members even at that time.

Chuen Shang was the youngest of four daughters, and a Buddhist and a vegetarian who relied mainly on astrology for her divinations. She had also been taught palm and face reading by her father. "At least 100 parts of the face are linked to a man's fate," the old man interjected at one point in the interview. He would later add, with obvious pride, that William Lessa, author of the classic *Chinese Body Divination*, had once been a pupil of his. "Face reading, ear reading, head reading—all give clues to a man's future paths," he told me. "Like the practice of medicine, *swan min* requires wisdom and experience." Several plaques and trophies displayed in the anteroom attested to the old gentleman's fame as a master calligrapher. Seeing my interest, he quickly reiterated a long-held conviction of his, that creativity and clairvoyance often go hand in hand.

This certainly seemed to be the case in his family; despite her youth Chuen Shang was a widely acclaimed artist, with her paintings of flowers and landscapes hanging in homes and galleries in many parts of the world. She told me she used her intuitive powers in her painting as well as her interpretation of the astrological signs.

The Shangs believed that both Oriental and Western students of the stars would inevitably arrive at the same predictions, though the culture of each had its own particular role to play in the interpretation of the signs. As we parted Chuen Shang told me, over the screaming of the Mina birds, that the first fortuneteller in the world might well have been a Chinese, Kuei Kel Tse, said to have lived sometime in the first millennium B.C., and known by his peers as a master of *swan min*.

There were the customary smiles and bows as I was led back through the courtyard to the red-lacquered door. The Shangs bade me good fortune and happiness as I stepped out into the vibrant world of Taiwan's capital. I'd learnt little of Chuen Shang's inner life, little of her "life of the mind." But I felt she represented yet another example of the possibility of a genetic component in psychic ability...or did she once again merely offer proof that the parts of us that are encouraged will develop, and that we tend to imitate what we hear and see in our immediate environment?

Later that same afternoon I talked to a professor of psychology at the University of Taipei. He confirmed what I'd already been told: that the Taiwanese show little interest in the paranormal. *Swan min* is even considered something of a joke; as a result, there are few who practice it. "Go to Hong Kong; maybe you will find it there," was a typical rejoinder when I asked about the ancient art. Any reference to it was accompanied by laughter. Clearly, in Taipei there was no abundance of claims for a sixth sense; if researchers happened to chance upon evidence of such a faculty, they did not take it seriously.

At the Grand Hotel where we were staying, I found a copy of the writings of Buddha. Consulting it might be helpful, I thought, toward an understanding of the character of the Chinese people. I opened the book at random, and my eyes fell on this passage: "The world has no substance of its own. It is simply a vast concordance of causes and conditions that have had their origin solely and exclusively in the activities of the mind that has been stimulated by ignorance, false imagination, desires, and infatuation. It is not something about which the mind has false conceptions; it has no substance whatsoever. It has come into appearance by the process of the mind itself, manifesting its own delusions."

I could have been reading Mary Baker Eddy on Christian Science. How many seers from divers cultures, disciplines and centuries have arrived at the same conclusion?

Chapter 28

Hong Kong:
An Irish Mystic Passes Through

Now it was on to Hong Kong, with its population of eight million squeezed into 400 square miles and its clashing *mélange* of the old and the new, the East and the West—in short, of a mass of incongruities which gave to the atmosphere of the city a strange and thrilling electricity. Who is there who can enter Hong Kong harbor without feeling a sudden surge of excitement?

I telephoned a certain Dr. Jong at the Chinese University. He confessed that there was "little interest in the paranormal here, but reports from Mainland China indicate much interest there, with many people claiming to have kinetic powers and other paranormal gifts." This wasn't surprising when I thought about the tremendous interest in *psi* in the then-Iron Curtain countries. It seemed to me that, where few possibilities exist for ego-fulfillment through material attainment, people are likely to search out other, less material, avenues—though whether or not these reports of *psi* successes were accurate was open to discussion.

Despite the professor's reservations, I'd heard there were still some elderly Chinese women in Hong Kong who practiced *swan min*—although the practice was "not well thought of," since it was believed such practitioners preyed upon the ignorant and the superstitious. True or not, I can only pass along what I was told. Moreover, no one even seemed to know where these practitioners of *swan min* could be found.

One of Hong Kong's leading medical doctors, a Buddhist with a scholar's knowledge of art and music, happened to be an old friend of mine. I'd hoped he might be able to help me. I was to be disappointed. When I asked him who among the four million Chinese living in Hong Kong might possess verifiable psychic powers, the very subject elicited such a lack of interest from him that it was almost as though he hadn't heard me. I was reminded of the

Zen word *mu*, which is the third possible answer to a "yes or no" question, and translates as simply "unask the question."

I wasn't easily discouraged. I turned to one Nancy Bekhor, an articulate and charming Australian who worked with an organization in Hong Kong called the Vital Life Center. The center was a haven for persons seeking to develop their intuitive powers. "It has filled a need for many of the more advanced Chinese, since the traditional system of education does not encourage individual thought," Nancy told me when we met. "What could be more individualistic," she added, smiling, "than intuition?"

As luck would have it, the famed Irish mystic Ann Hassett was then on a round-the-world lecturing and teaching tour and had stopped off at the center in Hong Kong to visit Nancy. Mrs. Hassett preferred to be known by the name of "Acushala." Her avowed purpose in life was to reveal to people the untapped powers innate in their minds. An Irish psychic in Hong Kong was hardly what I'd been looking for, but I jumped at the chance to talk to someone of Acushala's proven powers.

"Would you like to speak to her?" Nancy Bekhor asked me.

"Yes," I answered eagerly.

And so the interview took place.

Acushala told me that her childhood in Ireland had not been a happy one. She had realized early on that she 'knew' things through some sixth sense; but such a 'knowing' was discouraged by those around her. For an acutely sensitive child, those years were bewildering ones.

When she was old enough to take charge of her life, Acushala made it her mission to teach others to develop their own knowing. She taught students to elevate their thinking and reach out and claim the powers they little realized they possessed. "It's all in the mind," the Irish psychic reiterated. "The answers are all within. I find that Chinese students are the most receptive to my ideas."

Acushala observed that most people saw themselves as helpless victims of causes outside themselves. In her work, she taught them to turn their thinking into positive channels and thereby to draw positive happenings into their orbit.

The old adage, "What you hold in your mind, you will meet in the marketplace," was a message I was hearing increasingly in every part of the globe.

Acushala told me she could look at people and 'see' the events of their lives and the influences surrounding them. She could not explain this unusual gift—this "sixth sense"—but she insisted we all have the same power if we but choose to develop it. There was a higher self that we must recognize and "listen to."

Acushala's next appointment had arrived, so we had to say goodbye. Her enthusiasm had been catching. She had made me feel that life's possibilities were infinite. She sent me on the next leg of my journey with a tailwind of high hopes.

Chapter 29

Hong Kong:
Philippino with Healing Hands

My next stop was Bangkok, Thailand's capital. The plane was delayed briefly; but this gave me a chance to talk to a Philippino healer named Shirla Soyao, who had been living in Hong Kong for over 30 years.

Shirla had been born in Manila. Her childhood had been a normal one until, when she was six, the Japanese invaded the Philippines and seized its capital. Shirla remembered being caught up in the anxiety and fear of that time. It would finally end; but afterward life would never be the same.

Fortunately for her, one of her grandmothers had been a well-known healer. Shirla remembered being cured of all manner of childhood injuries and diseases by the grandmother's special herbal mixtures. This woman's steadying influence helped her survive the traumatic years of the Japanese occupation. While still a very young woman, Shirla had left the Philippines to study acupuncture in Hong Kong. She had married happily and never returned to Manila. Her life, since she had arrived in Hong Kong, had been devoted to healing.

Unlike most psychic healers, Shirla was unaware of her paranormal abilities until the advanced age of 39, when the realization came to her that she had "healing hands." She now believed the gift had been there all along, and that she'd been using it without understanding its source.

Shirla told me she received much of her intuitive knowledge of people, and how to help them, through vivid dreams.

"Trance dreams?" I asked.

"No, normal sleep dreams."

"How can you distinguish intuitive insight from ordinary imagination?" I asked. "Are there any physical sensations that are different?"

"Oh, yes," she quickly replied. "I feel a strange sensation in my body, and I 'know.'" Shirla's voice radiated happiness as she spoke; she laughed with the easy unselfconscious laughter of a child. This healer felt distance had nothing to do with her healing energies, and she often healed over the telephone, without ever seeing the caller.

Shirla told me finally that all her healing work was done in the name of Jesus Christ. She asked only that her patients, be they Jew, Moslem, Buddhist or Hindu, "believe at that particular moment that this particular healing is done in Christ's name." Her stated goal in life was both simple and profound: to help others with the gift she had been given.

Chapter 30

Bangkok, Thailand: Logic and Illogic of Astrology

My next Far East stop was Thailand. It was somewhat out-of-the-way; but surely, I thought, there must be compelling manifestations of the paranormal in this legendary land.

An old friend, Pipat Vibulsiriwongse, had once told me about a medium living in Bangkok who, when she received messages while in trance, took on the physical characteristics of her controlling spirit. It seemed the controlling spirit had been a crippled old man who was well-known throughout Thailand in his lifetime as a statesman, and so was easily recognizable to those attending the seance. While in trance, the medium doubled over into a gnarled, twisted figure and spoke in a deep, croaking voice. Even her features altered to resemble those of her legendary control. So completely did the medium assume the dead man's identity, that her audience was startled when, at the end of the seance, she unwound from the spirit presence and assumed her normal appearance.

I thought how sad it was that her control couldn't have been a celebrated Siamese dancer! Would she then have become lithe and graceful while in trance? My speculations turned out to be fruitless; I learned that the medium had left Bangkok and no one seemed to know her whereabouts.

Maybe this was just as well, since I had only a brief time in what was once called the Kingdom of Siam, and I wanted to talk to one of Bangkok's leading astrologers, Yupayao Srivatamchae, about astrology—a subject I'd never really understood and hadn't even been planning to pursue on my round-the-world search for female psychics.

Yupayao was quick to confirm my belief that astrology had no place in a study of female psychics. This Bangkok resident had the dark-eyed delicate beauty and gentle manner for which Thai women were celebrated, and she spoke in a soft, slow voice, carefully enunciating every word. Practicing her craft in an international crossroads like Bangkok, she had clients from every corner of the world who represented every walk of life.

Even as a child, Yupayao had always been curious about the future and fascinated that there were people who knew how to predict it. She had looked into the various means by which these predictions could be made, and had decided astrology was the most consistently accurate—and the most logical.

Yupayao had soon come to regard astrology as a "science" which, if properly interpreted, could provide readings of the past and future and offer valuable advice and aid. She decided that she would undertake a serious study of the stars and their influences herself, and had persuaded a venerable old Thai master to take her as a pupil. She had never regretted this decision, and found her work increasingly fascinating.

Whether from a sense of modesty—or of honesty, or of neither—Yupayao told me many times that, "I'm not psychic. Reading the stars is a science. Reading the stars and interpreting their influence has nothing to do with psychic insight. It is a pure science, discovered many thousands of years ago, and it has proven its accuracy in the lives of many, many people.

"But, like any science," she continued, "it takes years of study to master. It is very difficult to learn. To interpret the astrological signs correctly, one has to consider the culture into which a person is born and his or her own individual family environment, career, marital status and life situation. A prince and a pauper born at the same moment will feel the same positive or negative influences of that given time; but the outcomes of the two lives will be vastly different. Under a certain sign, a prince might ascend to a throne; obviously, a pauper would have no such chance. Interpretations must be done logically."

Yupayao went on to explain that each star, as it moved through the heavens and changed its position, had a meaning and an influence in relation to a particular person or a particular time. "So you see," she said, smiling, "it becomes quite, quite complicated! And did you know that each star has a special relationship with earth, air, water, and fire?"

144

No, I hadn't known that; and I doubted if I would understand it even if she explained it to me.

"Remember," Yupayao pursued, "astrology always predicts general tendencies, and in some cases can even pinpoint happenings closely and accurately. For instance, by calculating the influences at the moment of a person's birth, on a particular day of a particular month, in a particular year and at a particular place, the astrologer will be able to deduce a person's past as well as future.

"It's interesting to note that there can be accurate predictions for countries as well as for people," she added. "For instance, at the founding of the Kingdom of Siam, in 1782, the astrologers predicted that a king would rule Siam for 150 years. In 1932, 150 years later, the monarchy ended and Thailand became a democracy, with the king thenceforth subject to the will of parliament."

I asked her about the specific ways in which the stars and their positions in the heavens could influence a person's life. "Remember," she cautioned me, "it is a person's feelings and behavior that are influenced, not outward circumstances. The outward circumstances are in turn influenced by the person."

"Give me an example," I asked. "Suppose a man wins a lottery."

After a moment's thought, she responded: "Ah, the stars had no say in which number would win, but they did have an influence on the man who purchased the lucky ticket. Do you see?"

I could accept that—maybe. "But how did the stars exert an influence in the first place?" I asked.

By this time, another astrologer had joined us. We'd been starting to talk about the human body—a mass that is nine-tenths water. "If the moon can pull the ocean around and influence the tides..." Yupayao had been saying musingly.

Was that her answer? I couldn't be sure, for by then the two astrologers were engaged in an animated and lengthy conversation in Thai.

If this was indeed the way the stars exerted their influence, what a field of study this was for future scientists, considering science's ever-growing ability to measure the brain's activity. I became lost in reflection on our partially-liquid brains and those ever-changing magnetic tugs whose presence Yupayao had been evoking. Certainly, as a part of the physical universe, we are constantly interacting with those magnetic fields, and in ways we can scarcely dream of.

"Oh, do forgive me, please," Yupayao said suddenly, turning back to me. "It's just that I have such difficulty explaining certain things in English. I'm not sure I've made you understand, but I can tell you that astrology has a very firm basis in science."

We said goodbye; and, pushing her silky black bangs back from her forehead, Yupayao reminded me one last time that, "Astrology is a science that takes years to master, and intelligence, of course, to use it correctly. But, no, there is no psychic element involved. It is a science!"

I was keenly disappointed I hadn't met the famous Bangkok medium whose control was said to be the deceased Thai statesman. I wondered if this experiencing of a control might not simply be a symptom of a rare disease that causes a loss of "propriorception;" that is, the sense that enables us to feel that all the parts of our body belong to us and that it is we who own and operate them. I knew that various forms of acute polyneuritis could cause this sense of proprietorship to be lost or severely impaired. Didn't the same thing happen to a medium when another entity took over? She could no longer sense her body as her own.

On the other hand, I doubted that polyneuritis was a disease that could come and go suddenly, at the whim of a shift of consciousness in its victim.

There had to be another explanation!

Chapter 31

Singapore, Malaysia: A Clairvoyant Who Seasons Intuition with Reason

Arriving in Singapore, I was startled to find that the colorful old Raffles Hotel had undergone dramatic renovations, though there were still the same vast bedrooms, still the same courtyard dark with weaving palms—still the same ever-shifting kaleidoscope of guests as diverse as all the races and cultures of the world.

I decided to first pay a visit to the venerable old "Writers' Bar," hoping to absorb one more time, as if I were a psychometrist, the vibrations left there by that roster of literary giants who still gazed down from faded photographs lining the walls: Noel Coward, Somerset Maugham, James Michener—even Joseph Conrad, though I'm told the author of *Lord Jim* had been practically a teetotler. In fact, I would have to content myself with these immutable presences; the few friends I'd known in Singapore were either dead or had moved on.

Many years before, I had come to this city with a letter of introduction from a Viennese friend to the aging Sultan of Johore. I had spent a fascinating afternoon in his magical jungle kingdom 16 miles outside of Singapore, and at that time had met the Sultan's grandson, who now bore the title. But I didn't feel I could call him up after 30 years to ask for the name of a female soothsayer.

No; here in Singapore, I was on my own.

My independent stance led to a serendipitous happening. Searching through the pages of the telephone directory on the off chance I might come across the word "psychic," I caught sight of a listing for a "Psychological Testing Center." Thinking this center might be some help, I dialed the number. When I explained to the psychologist in charge, Elaine Liu, exactly what I wanted, she responded in a surprised tone: "How on earth did you happen to call me?"

"Oh, entirely by chance," I answered. "Why?"

After much embarrassed laughter, she confessed, "Well, I hesitate to recommend myself, and I don't usually talk about these things—I certainly don't talk about them around here—but I randomly exhibit the gift of *psi* myself." There was a brief silence; then she said in a low voice, "Come tomorrow, and we'll talk."

Elaine Liu had offices in the Colombo Center, a handsome new building some blocks from the winding Singapore River. She was a highly trained professional, and so I could understand why, working as she did in a field where scientific methodology was the yardstick, she rarely talked publicly about her paranormal gift. I felt quite privileged she was willing to discuss with me this intriguing facet of her mind.

Elaine turned out to be small of stature, with agreeable features and skin as smooth as bisque. Born in Malaysia, she'd been brought to Singapore while she was still quite young.

Her parents, who had been educated by Christian missionaries, were both scholars, and placed a great deal of emphasis on "higher learning." They had sent Elaine to England to do her graduate work in psychology.

Despite advantages such as these, Elaine's childhood had not been a happy one. "There were frequent quarrels in the family, making for many difficulties," she told me. "These very difficulties, however, in retrospect I feel enabled me to become strong." As a young girl in Singapore, Elaine attended many churches of various denominations, eventually converting to Catholicism.

She had first become aware of her potential as a psychic when she began to have vivid dreams with prophetic content. Given her training, she was often able to understand their symbolism and to act on the information implicit in them. Other times, she would have sudden intuitive insights while in a waking state; these were usually accompanied by a strong, uncomfortable feeling in the area of her solar plexus. Elaine felt that these dreams protected her— and in some cases enabled her to protect others.

She believed that experiencing *psi* without enough knowledge to understand what was happening could be highly confusing to the person. She urged those who possessed *psi* abilities to develop their reasoning faculties as well. In that way, she was sure, they could then use their paranormal abilities more effectively.

Elaine's professional career was that of a psychological evaluator and counselor. She felt that, because of her sufferings as a child, she was better able to understand the problems of her patients. When people came to her for help, they often had no idea what lay at the root of their difficulties. When her random psychic insights clicked in during counseling, Elaine was able to unerringly sense where those areas of conflict lay, and to provide immediate help to the patient. "You have to remember, though," she cautioned, "that there is always a unique vibration between the psychologist and the patient, and that this can affect the results."

Elaine felt that persons with psychic ability were under an imperative to maintain a state of personal purity. "This is the surest way to develop the talent," she asserted. We laughed when we found ourselves both beginning almost simultaneously to quote from Saint Paul's *Epistle to the Philippians*: "...and comprehend with all Saints what is the length, breadth, depth, height."

"Oh yes, all knowledge is *there*," Elaine reiterated, "and our innate ability to tap into it will surface as we become more and more in tune with the universe."

Elaine's declared mission in life was to help others. "So many people aren't really living," she told me. "They're simply existing. They haven't even begun to guess at their possibilities. I try to help people with their personal growth and development, to eliminate their blockages and enable them to realize their potential."

We discussed Icelandic educator Erlendur Haraldsson's belief that the fewer defenses a subject has, the "stronger his psychic power." And we wondered: Could this mean that our emotional blocks, and the coping mechanisms we have developed, are short-circuiting our sixth sense?

I asked Elaine: "If man is the product of endless variables—his chemical reactions, his genetic makeup, his unique prenatal endowment, his particular parents, his early brainwashing—shouldn't this cause us never to take another human being too seriously, and to have a sincere sympathy for all?"

Elaine agreed that brainwashing occurred from the moment of birth until roughly the age of seven. "The conditions for it are optimal," she affirmed. "You have dependency, the near-blank state of the mind, the presence of alpha brain waves only. These factors place individuals in a receptive state for the varieties of contradictory information that are constantly bombarding them. It's no wonder there are emotional blocks to be removed, defense mechanisms to be seen for what they are, emotional tangles to be unsnarled. We certainly shouldn't be surprised that the individuals themselves have little understanding of the root causes of all of this."

Elaine left me with as many questions as she did answers. I wondered, do our emotional blocks prevent us from perceiving other realities? Have we constructed defense mechanisms against our own spiritual growth?

It seemed as if the situation of merely being human militated against the development of psychic powers.

How, I wondered, could we ever get around the vicious cycle of our own vulnerability preventing us from accessing those very powers which would protect that vulnerability?

I hoped that, in the days to come, I would soon begin to answer these questions.

Chapter 32

Bali, Indonesia:
Witchcraft Among the *Dukins*

During the long flight to Indonesia, I continued to wonder how long we can all blithely ignore a phenomenon just because it makes us feel uncomfortable. Those individuals who have sudden unexplained insights have either stumbled upon a hitherto undiscovered law, or else they have brains more highly evolved than those of the rest of us. If this is indeed the direction man's evolution is taking, shouldn't such activities be encouraged?

The part of the world I was flying over was certainly one where the traveler was forced to ponder the dynamics of evolution. Why, for instance, did so many flightless birds evolve in New Zealand? Was it because there were no predators there to cause them to develop their wings for escape, and so their vestigial wings atrophied? We know that when New Zealand broke off from Gondwanaland—aeons ago, during the Paleozoic Age—mammals had not yet appeared on the evolutionary ladder, and they *never* appeared indigenously in New Zealand. Obviously, different influences had led to different directions in development.

What caused marsupials to appear in Australia and New Guinea rather than in other parts of the world? Why did the platypus appear only in Australia, or the snow leopard only in India? Fortuitous influences had to be the answer. But now, influences need not be so fortuitous. With his present knowledge, man can begin to influence his own evolution.

My thoughts were cut short by a voice announcing we were landing in Denpasar, Bali's capital. I had been coming to the island of Bali for over thirty years, but each time I was struck anew by its assault on the senses--all *six* of them. The delicate trance dancers, the dark tales of demons, the temple priests, the chattering monkeys, the scent of the red jasmine tree, the haunting music of the gamelans—all of these conspired to touch some unplucked cord in

151

the soul of even the most down-to-earth pragmatist. There was a dreamlike quality that pervaded the island of Bali, one it was impossible to shake off. "Surely," I thought, "I will hear of very different visions here."

During my previous visits, I had always stayed with Tjokorda Agung, Prince of Ubud, and his three wives, in their palace in the center of the village. After Tjokorda's death and his ceremonial cremation, his elder son, Putra, had received the title; it was with him and his pretty young wife that I now stayed. Putra seldom wore the sarong, and was more attuned to Western ideas than his father, but he had inherited something of the old man's easy native charm and had left the palace relatively unchanged. There were some notable differences, however: Electricity, albeit of the weakest current, had replaced the dim oil lamps; and there were spasmodic outbursts of running water in the bathing area. There was no telephone as yet, but further gestures toward modernization were promised for the future. There were still the same high ceilinged pavilions, still the same gilded doors, still the same carved stone demons in the gardens, still the occasional gecko hurrying up the white mosquito netting covering my bed.

I felt quite at home—particularly when I heard that Gusti Barata was still in the neighborhood. Barata was the prince's cousin, and he was knowledgeable in all areas and always a reliable source of information.

"Yes," he assured me when, on my second day, I put the question to him. "We have women of that sort, who know things in some other way."

He told me that in Bali it was the witch doctors, or *dukins* as they were called, who were said to possess paranormal powers— and once again a genetic component was indicated, for I was also told that such powers tended to appear in several generations of the same family. The *dukins* not only healed illnesses but they acted as marriage counselors and arbitrators. This 'counseling' did not consist of advice and mediation, but of the use of prayer and holy water to turn discord into harmony—to heal rifts, to end feuds. I took all this on advisement. It was difficult to keep an open mind

152

on an island where superstition was rampant, but you had to listen, and I did.

I engaged a driver, and an attendant from the palace to act as an interpreter. In a car of uncertain vintage, whose most notable feature was a strip of blue linoleum covering the floor boards, we set out after a hard rain in search of the local *dukin*.

The car lurched out of the courtyard into the main street, dodging potholes and careening cyclists as we gathered speed. Out in the open countryside, the terraced rice paddies reflecting the sky on either side, we charged furiously down the main road toward the little village of Wanaui, our driver slowing down only to swerve around an occasional chicken or sleeping dog. The village came into sight; three small girls balancing temple offerings on their heads waved shyly as we bolted by. We took a sharp turn to the right and plummeted down a steep, muddy road; several hundred yards more and a turn to the left, and we had come to the simple straw-roofed house of Ibu Wayan Ginada, the village *dukin*.

Ibu was a handsome woman of great dignity who was still in her early forties—quite a young age for someone of so respected a calling. Though her feet were bare and her soiled sarong faded and worn, she received us with ceremonial formality. She quickly spread out a bamboo mat and motioned for us to sit down. An assortment of scraggly dogs were climbing over our legs and scratching themselves between bouts of spiritless barking; Ibu firmly slapped them away and called to her son to bring coffee. Despite the rumpus, she was in complete control, her personal power evidenced by her luminous eyes that flashed fiercely in the sunlight as she gazed at us.

I learned that Ibu Wayan Ginada had been born on the Indonesian island of Nusapenida, off the coast of Sanur. When she was still a small child her parents had moved to Bali, where her father had been a servant in the royal household of Klungkung. After both her parents had died, within a few years of each other, she was kept on at the palace as a servant. When she reached adulthood, she made the trip to Bali's capital. There she remained, eventually marrying a young soldier on duty in Denpasar.

A mysterious event changed their lives. One day, a small Balinese dagger known as a *kris* appeared without explanation in the household. No one could account for its presence, and Ibu's husband could not stop worrying about what this visitation might mean. He became gravely ill, and during his illness he heard a voice telling him, "Look after the *kris* and pass it on to your wife, so that she may heal you." The husband did this, and he immediately became well.

Ibu Wayan Ginada's husband completed his military service and retired from the army to work in the rice paddies of Wanaui. From that point on, Ibu told us, she found herself able to cure a variety of illnesses. She had had little education and she had no knowledge of medicine, but she prayed a great deal, and she was soon able to bless water and oil which then acted as healing agents. "Buddhists and Christians as well as Hindus come to me," she said. "They must want only to be healed."

Ibu not only cured illnesses, but she could also take away bad fortune and spells that had been cast over people by practitioners of black magic. "When the disease comes out, I know it has happened, for I feel very close to the gods," she explained.

There was a small family temple in the modest compound, inside of which stood an altar. Upon this altar the mysterious *kris* was laid, along with offerings of food, flowers and incense. Ibu declared that it was her mission to pass this healing power on to her six children and to other members of the village.

"It's not a profession; it's not for money," she explained to me in parting. "It is a gift."

She followed us to the gate and pressed her hands together in a gesture of farewell. The scraggly dogs were barking again, and two roosters had begun scuffling noisily in the muddy road outside. Ibu seemed oblivious to her surroundings; as she waved good-bye to us, hers was a look of surpassing tranquillity.

There would be no way I could assess her claims. But the compelling dignity of her presence had somehow transcended the humble surroundings; this was the memory of her I would carry with me forever.

Chapter 33

Columbo, Sri Lanka: *Manyos* Who Channel Unilingual Spirits

My next flight took me over the Indian Ocean to Sri Lanka, a land I will always think of as Ceylon. It was well after midnight when I arrived at Colombo's old Galle Face Hotel. I had stayed there in the 1950s, and I had to confess to an odd experience of *déjà vu* as I approached it by the North Road and caught my first glimpse in many years of that monumental old relic rearing up ghostly and silent beneath the full moon.

The red carpets were worn and the ancient lift groaned as it struggled upward. A wizened old porter led me down a tall, narrow corridor, gesticulating about him as he went. "But look, Madam," he proudly announced, "do you know we have air-conditioning now?" This was certainly true: a blast of cold air struck me as I entered my enormous room overlooking the sea, with its heavy Dutch furniture an insistent reminder of Sri Lanka's colonial past.

There are women in Sri Lanka called *manyos* who are considered to be oracles. These female psychics spend their lives providing answers to the questions that are brought them. Some *manyos* even cure physical and mental ills, though the means by which they do so are not yet understood. The majority of such women take a vow never to marry; they believe that if they do their powers will instantly vanish.

I had heard of a particular *manyo*, a Mrs. Jayasinga, who lived near the village of Talahana Koswatta, and I assumed from her name that she had not taken the vow. There was no way of advising Mrs. Jayasinga in advance of my coming, so I decided simply to appear on her doorstep and take my chances. On the following day, a driver and an interpreter arrived at the hotel to fetch me for the journey—both of them very excited to have an excuse to visit the house of a *manyo*.

155

It's a fact of life in Colombo that no one ever drives slowly. Once a vehicle is set in motion, it seems to be mandatory that it travel at full speed, that it never slow down, and that it clear from its path with ceaseless ear-splitting blasts of the horn every possible obstacle until its destination is reached. As we tore out of Columbo toward the highway leading south, passenger buses, street rallies, saffron-robed priests, a ragged file of cows, all scattered frantically before us as we pounded down the last crowded street and were finally free of the city.

Once beyond the Sri Lankan capital, our driver, his battle won, took his hand off the horn and shifted to an almost reasonable rate of speed which would last for the duration of the journey. I sank back in exhaustion. The interpreter, releasing his frightened grip on the seat in front of him, introduced himself as Mr. G. E. Vandort, of both Indian and Dutch descent.

Mr. Vandort was a man of some education, and furthermore a communicant of the Catholic Church; nevertheless, he voiced a grudging respect for the phenomenon of the *manyo*.

"The genuine ones do a lot of good for certain people," he told me. Mr. Vandort felt, though, that in many of the cases of "supernatural" healings, the patient's belief in the cure was the sole effecting agent. This admission led Mr. Vandort to further reveal that his own interest in the *manyos* was entirely a function of his curiosity about the unused powers of the human brain and the general need for a more unbiased investigation of those powers.

Mr. Vandort explained to me that traditionally the *manyos* were supposed to grow into their powers of prophesying through the practice of a pure life. The calling of clairvoyant and prophet was a high one; only those who were spiritually elevated were considered worthy of it. Not only did the *manyos* provide answers and diagnose and heal illnesses; they were also able to exorcise spells cast by practitioners of the evil arts.

All in all, as the conversation went on, I was becoming increasingly eager to meet one.

Now we were driving along a dusty road lined with Dutch *boerderij* farmhouses, small plaster huts, and the occasional Buddhist *stupa* jutting up half-hidden from an undergrowth of palms. A crudely printed road sign pointing left to Talahana Koswatta came into view—and, after only one wrong turning, we came to a stop in front of Mrs. Jayasinga's house.

An ancient automobile, completely without tires, stood in the pathway, while several small children, teasing a cat, blocked the doorway. When we had finally gained entrance, Mr. Vandort explained to the *manyo*'s husband in Singhalese the reason for our unexpected visit. The moment the interpreter finished, every door in the small receiving room flew open and a dozen pairs of intently curious eyes peered out at us in silence. We had become the objects of an unabashed and searching scrutiny.

"The *manyo* is resting," her husband told us. "But wait, she will come soon and speak with you."

We seated ourselves on two wooden chairs near the entrance, and waited. Sooner than I'd hoped, a small, slender woman with graying hair, deep-set eyes and sharp features slipped quietly into the room. She might have laid claim to a certain distinctive beauty had not several of her teeth been missing; her determined efforts to conceal their absence had lent her mouth a certain awkward tilt.

Even as such stories went, Mrs. Jayasinga's turned out to be unusual. As a child she had been deeply "spiritually minded." But her family history was without seers of any sort, and there had been nothing whatsoever to prepare her for the occurrence which would transform her life: She had had a severe fall at the age of ten, which had injured her head, knocked out four teeth, and left her completely unconscious.

"As I began to regain consciousness," she told me, "I felt myself slipping into a trance state in which I 'knew things.' Since that time I've been able to re-enter that state at will, and I'm then able to speak on any subject." Mrs. Jayasinga added, "Afterwards, I remember nothing I have said."

"Are there any physical sensations?" I asked.

"Yes. I feel absolutely lifeless."

Her husband assured me that the people who asked her questions while she was in this trance state swore they always received accurate answers. He explained that his wife did not have a spirit guide as such, but that, inexplicably, she always 'heard' the answers in Tamil—a language that in her normal waking state she did not understand; Mrs. Jayasinga was monolingual and spoke only Singhalese. Her ability to understand a language she had no knowledge of had been enough in itself to make her an object of wonder in the village.

Mrs. Jayasinga told me she felt that through her work she had grown even more spiritually minded. She asked no money for the help she provided, and any small offerings her petitioners insisted on giving, she passed along to the temple. "It is used only for spiritual work," she explained. "I never buy food for the family with it."

I was eager to learn more about how the blow to her head had affected her. But someone from a neighboring village had arrived with a question. I was invited to witness the trance session in which Mrs. Jayasinga would supply the answer. We took off our shoes and went into the small family temple next to the house. It proved to contain a narrow altar laden with flowers, rice cakes, incense, and replicas of various Hindu deities.

The *manyo* stood before the altar, repeating an inaudible mantra over and over again. Finally, she gave a terrible gasp and collapsed into the small chair beside the altar. Two women knelt on the floor in front of her. The one with the question spoke quickly: She had lost her watch and wanted to know if she would ever find it again. Eyes closed tight, the *manyo* pronounced: "You will get the watch back in ten days."

The questioner pressed her for more information. The *manyo* hesitated; then, slowly shaking her head, she said: "It is your own son who has stolen it!"

The poor woman became visibly agitated. She began to ask questions about the son. The *manyo* shook her head vigorously. "Only one question at a time," she said firmly. "I have told you about the watch. If you want to discuss your son, you must come back. Only one question at a time."

The answers had been given in Tamil at first, then in the same tone of voice translated by the *manyo* into Singhalese. The trance over, the *manyo* returned to her original smiling state, her lips as ever stained to a bright magenta by the beetle nuts she was fond of chewing. Mrs. Jayasinga seemed totally unaware of what had taken place, while the petitioner, visibly shaken, placed a few rupees on a beetle nut leaf beside the altar and quickly tiptoed out.

I'll never know the fate of that purloined watch, but I will be forever haunted by memories of that dusty village in the south of Sri Lanka—memories that raised unanswerable questions in my mind, such as: If the son indeed stole his mother's watch, how did the *manyo* know? Why, if the *manyo* spoke only Singhalese, were her answers given in Tamil? Would the *manyo* have possessed a paranormal gift without the blow to her head—or had the accident opened up some untapped area in her brain?

Perhaps the woman who lost the watch knew, on some subconscious level, that her son was dishonest. Perhaps the *manyo* had vaguely sensed that knowledge, and simply made an educated guess.

Chapter 34

Pondicherry, India: At the Ashram of
Sri Aurobindo and The Mother

My next stop was Madras, a huge and bustling seaport in south-east India. It would be the starting point on my journey to the famous ashram of Aurobindo, in Pondicherry, some 200 miles down the coast.

At a time when such practices were highly unusual in India, the ashram of Aurobindo had been one of the first to accept women devotees. I had wanted to find out what I could expect there, so I questioned psychologists at Madras University before leaving.

One of these scholars expressed a belief contrary to that of most Western thinkers. He was convinced that man's brain is already fully evolved—that all the potential is there and that man's subsequent evolution will be realized as he discovers and develops his present inborn capacities. "Man's physical brain will not change," this psychologist told me. "It will simply be more and more fully utilized." The ashram at Aurobindo was expressly dedicated to the cultivation of just this kind of evolution.

Hearing these words made me all the more anxious to get started on my journey. Some miles down the coast, I turned inland from the Bay of Bengal; I wanted to stop first at the village of Kanchipuram, on the off chance there might be women devotees at the small ashram located at the center of the town.

The ashram lay on a very narrow, very crowded street. I got out of the car, threaded my way through a file of unruly goats, slipped off my shoes, and quietly entered the building. The hall with its lofty ceiling offered a welcome respite from the oppressive heat. The street noises faded into silence. Several older scribes, wearing only cotton *lungis*, sat lotus-fashion on the cool tile floor, writing intently in tall ledgers placed before them. They peered up in unison as I passed, nodded a solemn greeting, then returned to their work, taking no further notice of my presence.

160

A tall priest, his forehead marked with ash, entered from down a long corridor. He bowed gravely and informed me that the guru was sleeping. "You can imagine," he explained, "that the guru, at age 95, needs plenty of rest."

I asked if there were women devotees at this ashram.

"No, no," he murmured, with an air of disapproval. "At this ashram there are no women. At the one in Pondicherry, now, there you will find women. But there are no women here, no!" He bowed again gravely; I took my leave, retracing my steps past the row of scribes who once again nodded to me in unison. I retrieved my shoes, renegotiated the goats, and climbed back into the car, all the while followed by the curious stares of the huddled knots of vendors crowding the narrow street.

It wasn't long before I was in Pondicherry. This is a small, unhurried seaside city—and something of an anachronism on the Indian landscape, since it was ruled by the French until the 1960s and still retains the flavor of a French provincial town of a century ago, along with the leisurely pace of that era. There were houses whose architecture was distinctly Napoleon III; there were dapper French restaurants; there was even a self-styled Grand Hotel d'Europe, boasting exquisite French *cuisine* and ten fine rooms each one of them equipped with mosquito netting.

I didn't need to avail myself of the Grand Hotel, though; fortunately, I had been allowed to stay in one of several guest houses that the ashram has put aside for the accommodation of pilgrims. The guest house proved to be of the utmost simplicity, sparsely furnished, facing the sea and its cleansing breezes, and with an atmosphere of complete tranquillity. Guests were asked to speak softly and not slam doors or run water needlessly; large photographs of Sri Aurobindo, the ashram's founder, and of a woman called The Mother, gazed down from the walls of every room as if to remind us gently of these rules.

From the moment I arrived at the ashram of Sri Aurobindo, I heard the same refrain: "But how sad that you did not come sooner, when The Mother was alive! She was very, very psychic." I learned that The Mother was French, and that she had been an accomplished painter and musician in France before obeying a directive "from within" to come to Pondicherry and study and work with Sri Aurobindo. There had come a point when the Master had withdrawn into a life of seclusion and meditation; it was at that point that the Frenchwoman had taken over the direction of the ashram. She had come to be known by her adoring followers only as The Mother.

I was allowed to speak with one of these adoring followers on the morning of my arrival. This was a plump, middle-aged Indian woman who wore a simple cotton sari and no adornment of any sort except for a red *bindi* in the center of her forehead. She agreed to be interviewed only on condition that I not mention her name, as such a mention might "appear to be attracting attention" to herself; The Mother had discouraged all displays of vanity. When I agreed to honor this devotee's request, she spoke freely of the work of the ashram and her own personal history.

She had been born into a Hindu Brahmin family in Bombay. As a child, she had had strong spiritual insights and yearnings. She had loved to slip away in the light of the early morning to pray in the stillness of the temple, where, she told me, "the scent of flowers, the incense, the sandalwood, evoked in me feelings of intense happiness." Even at this early age, she had begun to ask questions like 'How is it we have come to be here?' and 'Why are we here?'

"As I grew older," this devotee recalled, "it became harder and harder for me to tolerate the noise, the traffic, the materialism of Bombay, with its people all trying to maximize their desires." Seeking a less hectic life, she abandoned the successful business career she was pursuing and entered the ashram at Pondicherry at the age of 35, in search of what she could only describe as 'something.' After only two days of meditation and prayer, she was sure she had found here what she was seeking, and made the decision to remain at the ashram for the rest of her life.

"Of course, one is always free to leave at any time," she explained to me. "There are no fixed rules or disciplines. We are all at different stages of development, and we must progress at our own pace."

Throughout our conversation, she often quoted The Mother. "The Mother was very, very psychic, much more so than me, and when we had a question she directed us to go within to find the answer. She stressed the importance of developing one's psychic potential in order to guide the self and others."

Along with meditation and prayer, my interviewee now devoted much time to the education of children. "The Mother taught that education for personal growth is far more important than mere education toward a job or profession. She taught that this should be undertaken at a very early age. Over 500 children are under the tutelage of the Ashram."

The devotees at the ashram believed Sri Aurobindo and The Mother had shared a strong metaphysical link during their lives. This closeness was illustrated by a fascinating story that had become one of the legends of the ashram. At Sri Aurobindo's death, a mysterious light filled the room. The light lasted several days, during which time Aurobindo's body was said to have shown no signs whatever of change or deterioration. Then The Mother had declared—before it was discernible to the grieving devotees gathered around the bed—that "the light is going out now." Only then did she allow the disciples to bury him.

I would have found it difficult to accept this account of the unchanged condition of the deceased guru's body if I hadn't recently read about the strange case of Sri Paramahansa Yogananda, a case well-documented by the director of the Forest Lawn Memorial Park, in Glendale, California. This celebrated Indian swami, who lived and taught in America and was the author of the famed *Autobiography of a Yogi*, died in Los Angeles, on March 7, 1952. Twenty days went by, and there were still no visible changes in his body! According to a report signed by impartial witnesses, the body had appeared to be "in a phenomenal state of immutability, no odor or decay, no visible disintegration at all." When the swami was finally buried, the case was declared to be "unparalleled" in the annals of burial history.

I was brought back from my musings by the devotee's further accounts of The Mother's teachings: "The Mother firmly believed that we are at a turning point in the world's history and that 'the reign of spirit will soon replace the reign of mind and matter.'

"She sought to inspire her female followers by reminding them that a woman's highest role has always been that of spiritual reformer and educator. 'Women's responsibility now is awesome,' she often told us. 'Women are capable of transforming the world.'"

It seemed The Mother had been something of an enlightened futurist. The devotee referred me to her writings where she said that "Nature is now feeling one of its great impulses to create something entirely new—something unexpected— and it is to this impulse that we must answer and obey. The ingredients are here now, in the human brain. The new race will be governed by direct perception of the Divine Law within."

These words made me wonder what would happen if paranormal abilities became accepted, and cultivated, and encouraged. What if they appeared with increasing frequency in future generations, until they became the norm? What effect would this have on the life of mankind?

Certainly it would be a very different world.

"How is the intuition developed?" I asked the devotee.

She answered that, according to The Mother, intuition was developed by cultivation of the inner self. "When the mind is still," The Mother had written, "the light of truth shines and gives birth to intuition. Those who are accustomed to listening to this voice out of the silence take it more and more as the instigating factor in their actions; [they are] guided through the windings of life by this superior instinct, as by a strong, unfailing hand."

The Mother believed that the psychic factor, which we consider almost abnormal now, will certainly be quite normal and natural in the mankind of tomorrow. "Intellect will not be sufficient for him," she wrote. "To discover and set free this greater power within shall henceforth be his great preoccupation. Man's aim shall finally be...to become himself."

There was a great commotion outside the ashram; new pilgrims were arriving. There were hurried introductions all around; then it was time for me to leave.

The devotee, her dark eyes glowing, clasped her hands together in farewell. As we walked to the door she stopped to remind me once again, "Remember, my dear, we, here at the Ashram, live quite simply, with only a minimum of necessities—the simplest food, the simplest clothing, the simplest shelter."

I could certainly understand that if you felt you were leading mankind toward its next evolutionary step such basic fare would be quite sufficient.

We have gone from *homo erectus* to *homo sapiens*, it occurred to me, and perhaps someday we will become *homo psychic*—hopefully, as a by-product of our growth in goodness.

Chapter 35

New Delhi, India:
Auras of Sanctity and Odors of Disease

Arriving back in Madras late in the day, I waited until the next morning to catch a flight to India's capital, New Delhi. I was scheduled to meet in Delhi with Dr. Ramesh Paramahamsa, director of the Institute of Psychic and Spiritual Research.

Dr. Paramahamsa was a broadly educated man who hoped his research would one day inspire the scientific community to take a closer look at paranormal phenomena. It seemed that in India, regardless of personal belief, the official attitude of the scientist must always be one of skepticism. Once again, I'd found *psi* on the defensive; once again, I had found it negatively described.

Dr. Paramahamsa had spent two decades studying various esoteric disciplines in Tibet. His treatise on the art of Ajapa Breathing as a path to psychic development was widely read and praised. I felt sure he would be in touch with women in Delhi professing metaphysical experiences.

I wasn't disappointed. He had chosen a particular one upon whom we should call, a Mrs. Krishna Kaul. We quickly set out by taxi to find her house. Mrs. Kaul lived in a far-flung part of the city; our drive was long and arduous, and our efforts at conversation were soon drowned out by the driver's pocket radio which, turned up to a deafening decibel, blasted out a dreary Indian ballad of rejection: *"He loves, she doesn't love him—."* I shouted some questions above the din, but Dr. Paramahamsa only shook his head and threw up his hands in a gesture of helplessness.

We eventually arrived and entered the enclosed grounds surrounding Mrs. Kaul's house. We were met by an elderly servant who led us up a flight of stone stairs to an open verandah. Mrs. Kaul soon appeared. She was a former Member of Parliament, a woman of great reputation in India, and known and respected for her strength and intelligence. She sat facing me on a long low sofa while, over a cup of tea I identified as the finest Darjeeling, we discussed her life and career. Mrs. Kaul's husband, a small compact man with a handsome face, soon joined us; he would add the occasional observation.

Mrs. Kaul had been born into a Brahmin family of Kashmiri origin; she had been the long-awaited child of adoring parents. "Eighteen years they waited," she exclaimed. "Can you imagine it? I grew up quite pampered, quite spoiled!" Her large gray eyes half-closed as she smiled over the happy memories of a childhood which, as she put it, had been "unmarked by any sadness."

Mrs. Kaul recalled that "quite early in my life, I somehow knew things before they happened. The gift was so apparent that my own mother would often ask me questions about the future. However, this was soon discouraged by other family members, who said, 'This is wrong; one shouldn't worry a child with such questions.' After that, my clairvoyance ceased to be a subject of discussion; it didn't fit into the pattern of their lives. I began to have ambivalent feelings about it myself.

"Even so, as I grew older the unsought insights continued to come, at unpredictable intervals and always on unpredictable subjects. These illuminations are usually preceded by a sleepless night, so that by now I have come to know when to expect them."

Mrs. Kaul married and moved to New Delhi, pursuing a life that was always blessed by good fortune. When her two children grew older, she decided to stand for Parliament, and won. Her main efforts during her six years in office were exerted on behalf of women. Mrs. Kaul's big gray eyes filled with tears as she talked about the burning of brides, about the perversion of the dowry practice, about the exploitation of young women. "Oh, life is hard for men too, I know, I know," she sighed, "but women are somehow more vulnerable, more defenseless."

Mrs. Kaul abruptly changed the subject to her ability to see a person's aura—of good fortune or of ill. "It's true," she insisted. "It's right there, on the forehead: a light or a cloud." With her acute sensitivity, she was even able to diagnose illness by the odor she picked up emanating from the victim.

By this time we had been joined by two unidentified gentlemen, both wearing the baggy pants-like *kurtas* of India and listening to every syllable with acute interest. "Him, there," Mrs. Kaul waved in the direction of one of the men. "He walked into my garden one day and I smelled something, a strange, greenish, sweetish odor. I knew at once that he was suffering from diabetes." Her diagnosis had been confirmed and the necessary treatment undergone. The diabetic smiled and nodded in confirmation; then he was summarily dismissed from the conversation as we returned to Mrs. Kaul's insights and future plans.

She was a strong believer in the value of higher education, and thought that intuition would develop as the intellect developed. "One must exercise the mind," she stressed. She hoped that one day soon she would re-enter the political arena: "There is so much to be done," she declared. Mrs. Kaul's eyes clouded over once again. "I only hope I can help a little. Reform is so difficult, always so many ramifications, so many long-held traditions, so many superstitions to be overcome." She threw up her hands and shook her head slowly.

The talk turned now to her children, a daughter living in southern India and a son living in Geneva. "No, no one else in the family seems to have the psychic gift," she told me in answer to my question. "We really never discuss it, you know. It's not something one discusses. But there are so many odd coincidences in life. How can one not recognize certain vibrations at work?"

The intense focus of her gray eyes suddenly became more diffused. She gazed quietly over my head into the distance, as if she were recalling something very important. I wanted to hear more, but it was past noon now, and we had to say goodbye. I left with the feeling that Mrs. Kaul, with her education, her intelligence, and her insight, was a woman well-equipped to be of great service to her country.

Thinking back over that conversation now, I marvel at the way in which degrees of sensitivity can vary from one individual to another. There are some individuals, I've been told, who are so highly sensitive they can comfortably tolerate only the dimmest light and the lowest noise level. For these persons the sensations of light and sound are amplified to an almost unbearable degree.

I was certain Mrs. Kaul's sense of smell was more acutely developed than most, and that her sight, which saw light and dark auras, must surely differ from yours and mine. We know that bees see colors that humans cannot. We know that dogs hear sounds that are inaudible to other species.

Where then does 'reality' actually lie? Always and only with the majority?

An intriguing incident took place on the ride back with Dr. Paramahamsa. Before dropping him off at his studio I showed him a snapshot of Barrie Stonehill.

"What can you tell me about this young man?" I asked.

He took the small photograph, looked at it for a long time, held it up and pressed it against his forehead, studied it again, and then said at last: "This man's mind works differently from anyone else's. This man has a completely unique mind." Dr. Paramahamsa had not said "body;" he had said "mind."

I could hardly wait to write to Barrie and tell him about this. I also wanted to tell him I had decided that any tests he underwent should be done in London. I was certain that there, on his home turf, he would feel more comfortable.

Chapter 36

Istanbul, Turkey: The Psychic Who Sensed the Prime Minister's Heart Disease

During my flight to Asia Minor and specifically Turkey, I thought about how sad it was that psychics were being examined by the wrong people. Who would be best equipped to test a mathematician? Other mathematicians, certainly. Perhaps psychics should be tested by psychics; a scientist who has never had a psychic experience is not well equipped to make a judgment about a psychic or create an open, sympathetic environment. As Carl Jung once said, "A thing which cannot be experienced may easily be suspected of non-existence."

My plane arrived at the Istanbul airport just at dusk. As our taxi neared the city, I heard the plaintive echoes of the Moslem calls to prayer and caught glimpses in the distance of the fading sunlight glittering off tall minarets and turning them to a rosy gold. Soon, we were weaving in and out of Istanbul's churning traffic, the air a miasma of exhaust fumes, edging our way inward toward the center of the city. We finally arrived at the old Yesil Ev Hotel, an oasis of tranquillity rising out of a beautiful garden behind the mosque of Santa Sophia.

Dining that evening with friends at an outdoor restaurant overlooking the shimmering Sea of Marmara, I decided that any description of Istanbul under a full moon should be left solely to the poets.

With only three days to spend in the city, I was fortunate on such short notice to be able to meet the psychic Sema Oztemir. Sema was always "quite booked," I'd been told, and it wasn't until the morning of the day of my departure from Istanbul that she telephoned me to say, "Yes, I will see you. Come in just after one o'clock."

A highly intelligent young woman named Nilgun Cumali had agreed to act as my interpreter. Close to the appointed hour, we set out together in a cab. Luckily, Nilgun knew the way; with surpassing calm she directed our driver through the tangle of traffic-congested streets. Suddenly she pointed to a white duplex rising above a busy corner. "There it is, I'm sure that's it!" she exclaimed.

We alighted quickly, so as not to stall the stream of cars and lorries crowding into the lane behind us. We went up a short flight of stone steps and found ourselves at Sema Oztemir's door.

The youthful Turkish psychic greeted us warmly. She led us into a small room where several people were sitting in silence: an old man who was fingering a string of amber worry beads, two dark-eyed girls who I presumed had come for readings, and a handsome young boy seated cross-legged on a large cushion on the floor. Sema made no effort at introductions; instead, she quietly invited us all to share a bowl of chocolates—hoping, I supposed, to establish thereby some sense of community among the group. Sema eased herself into a low, cushioned sofa next to the elderly man; above them on the wall hung a heavy gold leaf frame encasing a verse from the Koran.

"She's very pretty," Nilgun whispered to me, nodding toward a large photograph of Sema on the adjacent wall.

"She certainly is," I agreed, "and much younger than I'd expected. Is she Moslem?"

"I would suppose so," answered Nilgun. The bowl of chocolates was empty now. All eyes were focused in our direction.

I asked Sema Oztemir if her childhood had been a happy one.

She hesitated (later, I would understood why), finally answering in almost a whisper: "It was not so happy—there were some family problems."

She indicated that the subject was closed.

"When did you first realize you were psychic?" I asked.

Sema looked puzzled.

"I mean, when did you have your first psychic experience?"

She nodded and said, "It was just after the birth of my third child. One night, I got up to get a glass of water. As I was about to drink it I looked down into the water and saw the face of my little

171

nephew; it was covered with blood; doctors were standing over him. This vision in the water was so vivid that I called out to my sister who was spending the weekend with me: 'Look, look in the water, I think it's your son...There's something the matter with him.'

"'No, there's nothing there,' my sister called back, 'it's only a dream, go back to bed.' I drank the water and tried to sleep.

"The next day, my brother-in-law telephoned my sister, saying: 'Come quickly, our son has been hurt!' When I went to the hospital with them, the child was there just as I'd seen him, surrounded by doctors, his little face covered in blood. The doctors had the same features as those I'd seen in my vision.

"Three more times I saw things in the water...things that later happened. I began to feel somehow different...and to hear voices.

"My marriage was a happy one, but for some reason which I could not then understand and even now cannot explain, I knew that it must end. I knew that if it continued it would not be so happy. I would rather that it ended before this should happen. My poor husband was bewildered. I remember crying and crying and being very sad. I also knew I would soon have a serious operation. This was a difficult time.

"Though no one in the family before me had been psychic, more and more I realized I had been given a special gift. My friends urged me to use it. They encouraged me, and I found that I could help them with my visions. I began to read grounds from their coffee cups."

"Can you really tell something from that?" I asked, trying not to sound too skeptical.

Sema smiled. "Actually, it is only a means of focusing my thoughts, if you understand. One drinks the coffee—in a cup of Turkish coffee, there are many grounds at the bottom. Then one turns the cup over, lets it cool, and looks into the cup. I believe strongly in God, and always begin the reading with a prayer."

Sema's face seemed to change, to soften, as she talked. In the course of our conversation her dark eyes often filled with tears.

"She's very sensitive," Nilgun whispered.

Sema continued: "Even so, I still worried about giving these readings. Could it be somehow harmful? It was all so strange; you can understand how I felt. Then, one night, I had a dream. I was going down a flight of stairs and suddenly I saw a little man beside me who had a kind, gentle face. 'Don't worry,' he told me, 'you can't hurt anyone. I will help you in your work.' After that, I felt that someone—this little man—was actually guiding me, helping me. He was always there. I said no one else in my family was psychic. I meant in the past, because my daughter, my third child, after whose birth I had that first vision in the water—she is very psychic, like me."

"Do any physical sensations accompany your insights?"

"Oh, yes," she replied quickly. "At the back of my head I feel something like a strong electrical vibration—and often illuminations come quite unexpectedly, not just when I'm focusing on the coffee cups. For instance, one day I was watching television and the face of our Prime Minister appeared as he was making an important speech. I suddenly 'knew' he was gravely ill, something with his heart. The next day, my husband came running in with a newspaper. The headline read, **'Prime Minister Scheduled for Heart Surgery.'**

"Some four years later, my marriage ended. I had a nervous breakdown. I was very depressed. I began to pray to God in great sincerity and humility. I prayed and prayed every day, and, gradually, a feeling of peace came over me. I had a deep sense of tranquillity, and this has remained with me ever since. In my work, I try to help others—some readings, yes, but more to help people understand themselves."

"Do you think the world makes proper use of its clairvoyants?"

"Oh, no. There is much we could do to help the world." Her face suddenly brightened. She smiled at Nilgun, then at me. "Let me read your coffee cups. I want to see what's in store for you!"

Before we could protest that we had already kept her from her clients far too long, she jumped to her feet to prepare the coffee. The old man who was fingering the worry beads looked up.

"My father," Sema said with great pride, giving him an affectionate pat on the shoulder. Now I understood her reluctance to confess that her childhood had not been a happy one; she hadn't wanted him to overhear.

Sema returned with the coffee. We drank it quickly; new faces were beginning to appear in the room, eager for the psychic's attention. Sema took Nilgun's cup first, turned it over on its saucer, let it cool, then cradled it tightly in both hands. She closed her eyes and seemed to be praying or repeating a mantra. Minutes passed. She finally opened her eyes and spoke in a staccato voice. There were several minutes of rapid Turkish.

When she had finished giving the reading for Nilgun, Sema took my cup and repeated the prayers. Then she quickly turned in my direction and, eyes focused just above my head, began to articulate her pronouncements. Somehow, my future as laid out in rapidly spoken Turkish sounded vaguely ominous. I looked at Nilgun for reassurance. "Actually, it's pretty good," she whispered. "I'll translate it later."

New faces were appearing at the door. We rose to leave. Sema kissed us on both cheeks and bade us farewell and good fortune. She waved to us from the top of the stairs as we drove away.

What Sema had said about past events of my life was surprisingly accurate, and it will be interesting to see if her predictions for the future are on target. But Nilgun and I agreed that just how a psychic acquires such knowledge, and not the accuracy of her predictions, is really the question that has to be addressed.

All through the following day, I thought about Sema and her insights. Which of the insights of a good psychic are simply lucky guesses, I wondered, and which are merely broad-based statements subject to individual interpretation—and which are true paranormal illuminations? These were all crucial questions, ones which should command the attention of the finest minds of our time.

My thoughts keep returning to the scientists. Having always had the deepest admiration for their relentless pursuit of knowledge, I wanted to say to them: "Because this is shadowy and slippery terrain, it needs those among you with the brightest torches."

174

Chapter 37

Thessaloniki, Greece: Healer
in the Arms of Angels

Twenty-four hours later, I found myself strolling through the ruins of the historic Greek city of Ephesus, some 35 miles south of Izmir in Asiatic Turkey. I was wondering what memories might be encoded in the ancient monuments lining its dusty, marbled streets. Had psychics with a gift for psychometry ever run their hands over these stones? If so, what impressions might they have picked up from the vanished past?

On the drive to Ephesus, I had reread St. Paul's *Epistle to the Ephesians*, addressed to "those saints which are at Ephesus and to the faithful in Christ Jesus." There were three verses in particular that seemed to me to be germane to the subject of psychic power. Paul spoke of the Ephesians as having been given *prophets*, and he admonished them to "speak every man truth to his neighbor, for *we are all members one of another*." Earlier, he had told the Ephesians of his prayer for them, that they, "being rooted and grounded in love, may be able to comprehend with all saints what is the *breadth, and the length, and depth, and height*."

Many thinkers of a mystical bent, including in our era P. D. Ouspensky, have understood this passage as referring to four dimensions. I wondered if the early Christian Saints had indeed had a knowledge of the fourth dimension. Was the ability to "comprehend" this lost after just a few hundred years, when the demands of pure Christianity came to be perceived as too high a price to pay? What happened to this ancient power of healing? Did the root and ground of love dry up gradually and wither away into dogma? Did Christ become more an idea to worship than a guide to follow? Rather than change themselves, had it perhaps been easier for men and women simply to accept themselves as poor miserable sinners, with the debt for their sins forever paid by the death on the cross? To worship, to be deeply thankful, is one thing; to emulate is quite another.

A few humble souls have sincerely tried it, and their influence on the world has been profound.

I had wanted to go on to Konya, to see the dervishes in action and witness the strange and mysterious light that supposedly filled the room when these tribesmen of southern Turkey whirled themselves into ecstatic states. But Konya was a day's journey, and it would be another day back to the Aegean coast; and I still had to visit Aphrodesia before leaving Turkey and going on to Thessaloniki in Greece.

If luck were with me, I would find there the celebrated medium Biktwpia Ouziel.

While recrossing the Dardanelles back into Europe, I suddenly remembered St. Paul's *First Epistle to the Thessalonians*, in which he says, "Despise not prophesying." That was a comfort! And yet we're told throughout the scriptures to "beware of false prophets," to beware of "wizards that peep and that mutter." St. John the Divine also wrote to the faithful, to "believe not every spirit, but try the spirits whether they are of God, because many false prophets are gone out into the world."

This was not an easy subject to deal with!

Soon enough, I was in Greece, and on my way to the northern city of Thessaloniki, or, as it is frequently known, Salonika. On my arrival I telephoned Biktwpia Ouziel. A young man who spoke English answered the phone. I told him what I wanted; after several minutes, he returned to the line to say that if I would come at midday tomorrow, "Biki" would see me, and he himself would serve as my interpreter.

On the following day I set out for Maypokopdaatov Street where Biki lived. This avenue was located in an area of newly-constructed, tall apartment buildings, just outside the center of Thessaloniki. Arriving at Biki's flat at the stroke of noon, I was greeted by the young Greek I'd spoken to on the phone. He introduced himself as Anastasios, and invited me inside. The apartment was attractively furnished, with a medley of colorful paintings and exotic wall hangings adding still more to its character. We sat down and I explained my mission in detail.

A door opened and Biki appeared, slim, sun-bronzed, and wearing a blue cotton blouse and skirt and narrow Grecian sandals. She hardly looked 20, but Anastasios had told me she was 32. Biki grasped my outstretched hand in both of hers and smiled the warmest of greetings—a greeting enhanced by the strange, vibrant intensity that played about her small and delicate features.

I soon learned that her mother was Egyptian and her father Israeli. Her mother had been a well-known Egyptian medium, so that Biki felt that perhaps her gift was inherited—"Though one doesn't really know how these things come about," she cautioned.

She told me a story that was unusual even by the standards I was now used to.

When she was born, both of her feet had been turned inward at such an angle that as a child she had not been able to walk. One day, she felt a frightening presence in the room, and a strange sensation in her feet and legs, as if someone were touching them. Others in the room at the time said they also sensed an unseen presence. Suddenly, Biki stood up; her feet had straightened out, and she began to take her first steps. At the same moment, she felt she had "some strange power" deep inside her.

From then on, Biki's dreams became frighteningly vivid, and she was able to 'know things' about people, such as who was good and who was "not well-intentioned," and much more.

I wondered if this might have been an experience of the opening of the kundalini. Biki explained that a feeling of alienation had come with her new power. "I found it difficult to make friends like other children. I was a poor student at school, never studying the lessons. But in the final examinations I always came first."

She confessed that her childhood had not been a happy one, since she always felt she was "different." Biki married at 16 and gave birth to a son the following year. When she was 19, she met a woman who possessed the same power as she did. The woman recognized Biki's unusual gift and urged her to move to Athens where she could study mediumship. Biki agreed, and did so. The experience of her early school years repeated itself while she was there: Though she was inattentive in class and unwilling to study, Biki always came first in her exams. "The answers somehow just came to me," she said, her voice betraying no hint of pride.

At one point in her early 20s, before she had learned to use the strange power she possessed, Biki had become so severely depressed that she tried to end her life by throwing herself out a window several stories above the ground. As she jumped, she had felt a "presence"—someone, something—catching hold of her. She'd turned three complete circles in the air and then landed on her feet. People who witnessed the incident, running to her side, were amazed to find that she had suffered no injuries except for a slightly sprained ankle. From then on, Biki knew that she was "protected," and that she was meant to live and to use her power for good.

She related an incident which marked yet another turning point in her life. "One afternoon while I was taking a nap," she recounted, "I dreamt I saw an Indian who looked something like a king. He told me I belonged to the same order, the same family, as he did, and that he would help me throughout my life whenever I was sick or unhappy if I would help him be a better person and help others to be better persons. At first, I doubted he was real, and he told me, 'I will give you a sign so that you will believe me.'"

Shortly afterward, Biki developed a very high fever. Her mother became alarmed and took her to the nearby hospital. The doctor on call, examining Biki, could discover no cause for her illness. Suddenly, he exclaimed: "What's this?" An odd little circle had appeared on Biki's right shoulder. By the time she got home from the hospital, her fever was gone, and Biki knew she had gotten the sign that she had been promised.

I must have looked a bit dubious, for she immediately jumped up from her chair and came around to where I was sitting. She pulled her blouse down over her shoulder and showed me the circle.

"Since then," she finished her story, "when I do my work in a trance state, that Indian is my guide."

Biki's sole aim in her work was to help others. But, she emphasized, "I will never take money from those near me in my life—

close friends, relatives." In the case of other clients, she was guided by the Indian as to whether or not to charge them. "Before I answer the door, I always know, and on one day of each week—Friday—I never take money from anyone. But can't I give you something to drink?" she now asked.

Before I could protest, she sprang from her chair and rushed out of the room. Anastasios leaned forward and whispered in a confidential tone: "She really is incredible. For instance, she can always read my mind; she always *knows* what I'm thinking. These people are very different from you and me."

I could certainly agree with him there!

Biki came back with three large glasses of orange juice and sat down beside me. Was it just a coincidence—or did she somehow know that I seldom drink anything but orange juice?

"The Indian talks to me frequently," she continued, face growing tense as she now recalled an unpleasant period. "Four months before the death of my father, the voice said to me, 'Your father is dead.' But that's ridiculous, I thought; my father is very much alive. Four months later, at the end of a long bout with depression, my poor father hung himself. Years later—and this is significant from the point of view of the study of psychics—my mother came across some letters he had written to members of the family. They were all dated four months before his death—and on the precise day that the voice had spoken to me."

Biki was clairvoyant as well as clairaudient; she could "see things in water." Once, she had conducted an experiment in which she'd invited several people with the same gift to look into a glass of water. "We all saw the same thing!" she told me.

I asked my usual question: "Are there any physical sensations accompanying your illuminations?"

"Oh, yes, my head, it's as though my hair were being pulled. And here," she pointed to the solar plexus, "and my skin." She gave a shudder. "The sensations are really quite strong."

Biki revealed that ever since the tragic suicide of her father she had always known without being told when somebody close to her had died. She said that she often worked with the dying now.

179

At this point in our conversation, she left the room to answer the doorbell. Anastasios leaned forward again, "It's truly remarkable. If someone is unconscious, in a coma and near death, Biki can stroke the person's face and the person will regain consciousness before dying. She has really great powers."

Biki returned with a young Greek woman, born in Thessaloniki, whom she introduced to us as Eleum. Eleum had apparently come to Biki ten years before for help with a serious problem. When the problem was solved, Biki had asked her if she would like to stay, saying, "You can help me in this work." Eleum had been with her ever since.

"At the time, Eleum had no real power," Anastasios explained, "only a strong belief. But now she 'knows' and 'sees' many things herself. She can touch a person's hand and know what kind of person she is dealing with. She has become a medium herself."

"Now she is able to see the Indian as well," Biki added, "and is a great, great help to me."

With that, Eleum joined in the conversation. "It's a pity, Madame, that you can't stay to witness a trance," she told me, remarking that when Biki was in trance her whole face completely changed. "You don't recognize her, and she speaks in a man's voice. In a trance state, she can actually produce real fire—she has great power, great energy.

"But it is a difficult life. She has never had any fun like other young people. It's a very demanding gift, and Biki is so good. She wants so much to help people."

By now we had been joined by Biki's son. He was a slender youth, with a face of the type you see in early Egyptian wall paintings: dark eyes, strong features, a sensitive tapering chin.

"The Indian once asked me if I'd like my son to have this power," Biki told me as she introduced him, "but I said, 'No, I want him to enjoy being young. I want him to have his own life.'"

The boy laughed and gave his mother an affectionate hug.

The doorbell rang and another young woman entered.

Biki greeted this woman warmly and rushed off to the kitchen again, returning with coffee and a tray of small cakes this time.

When my presence had been explained to the new arrival, she came over and sat down beside me. "You're here to learn about Biki," she said. "She's a most remarkable person; she only wants to use her power to help people. She is a wonderful friend."

When I was leaving, I unwittingly introduced a sobering note into the conversation by asking Biki for her predictions about the future of the world. Her happy expression abruptly faded, and she slowly shook her head. Her predictions were grim indeed: she foresaw that a sort of Armageddon was imminent. "But those who are good," she explained, "I mean, those who have learned to love one another—they will survive."

What was it that St. Paul had written in that *First Epistle to the Thessalonians*? "But touching brotherly love, ye need not that I write to you; for ye yourselves are taught of God to love one another."

Chapter 38

Venice, Italy:
Dream of a Romanian in Exile

Early next morning, I was on the road to Treviso, Italy, where I would board a plane for Venice.

I suppose Biki's being half-Egyptian was in some indirect way responsible for my wandering thoughts that day on the subject of the importance of looking-glasses, or mirrors. The ancient Egyptians would never have been able to get light down into their tombs at Luxor without their reflectors made of polished metal; and, for artists in general, a looking-glass is an indispensable ally. When a painter looks at a painting in reverse through a mirror, any deviation from the "likeness" of the subject becomes instantly evident. If the artist has painted one eye higher than the other, or placed the nose off center, the reflected image will enable the artist to see the mistake.

I wondered what would happen if the combatants in an angry dispute were forced to face themselves in a mirror and shout their accusations and aspersions at their own reflection; wouldn't that neutralize a lot of their emotion? There would be a sort of "distancing" effect, as each adversary now viewed the scene as an observer. Perhaps, one day, all sensible ombudsmen will adopt this as standard practice. The dreaded Medusa of Greek mythology could not be looked at head-on; if she were, the observer was turned into stone. It was only by looking at her reflection in the highly polished shield of the goddess Minerva that Perseus was able to lop off the head of that fearful monster of antiquity. Not, of course, that looking into a mirror was always a positive thing: also according to the ancient Greeks, Narcissus gazed at his own reflection in the waters of a fountain for so long that he pined away and died—hence the origin of our word "narcissist." Hell itself may be no more than a mirror, a mirror in which we face the awful realization of how distant we were from what we could have been, of how far our likeness had deviated from the reflection of God whom it was our birthright to resemble.

When I had been in Rome the year before, a Venetian friend who knew of my growing interest in those who claimed to have the gift of prophecy had told me about a "charming Romanian" who "knew everything" and who was living just off the Grand Canal in Venice. I had taken him to mean that the charming Romanian 'knew' the events of the past and future and would have much to tell me about her intuitive insights. Eager for an interview, I telephoned her when I landed in Venice and asked when we might meet.

"I don't quite understand what it is you want to talk to me about," she told me, "but do come along tomorrow. I should be most pleased to speak with you."

The next day, following her directions, I soon found myself in a small fifth-floor apartment filled with mellowing old world treasures that imparted a sort of muted patina to the rooms. The view from the wisteria-covered terrace could have inspired a painting by Canaletto.

"May I offer you a glass of wine?" this handsome if aging woman asked me. "Or what would you like? Do sit down, my dear. You must be quite tired after such a climb."

As though on cue, a pretty dark-haired woman appeared bearing a tray laden with crystal decanters.

"My daughter thinks I must have a nurse with me now," observed my hostess. "I've not been so very well lately."

We exchanged news about our mutual friend; we bemoaned the rising inflation in Italy; and we praised the current exhibition of paintings at the Academia Museum. As we talked, I was captivated by her warmth and enthusiasm. Finally, I dared ask her, "When did you first realize you were clairvoyant?"

"I was *what*?" she exclaimed, her eyes widening.

"But you do have knowledge of or an interest in psychic phenomena, do you not?" I persisted.

"Not in the least!" She laughed her delightful laugh, "I never thought there was anything to all that. I'm much too practical."

But how could this be? I wondered. I rattled on quickly about my special interest, trying frantically to explain my presence and rectify what must have been a complete misunderstanding.

I'm sure that it was only to spare me further embarrassment that she now feigned curiosity in the subject, and listened with that flattering attentiveness which is so characteristic of those who know the world well. From time to time, she even nodded in grudging agreement.

She finally stopped me to ask a question—and then suddenly hesitated. "But wait," she said eagerly, "I can tell you something after all. I once had a most vividly prophetic dream, a dream that came true on the following day and changed the course of my life. In my dream, I saw myself climbing over a high wall. It happened just that way the next day, and led to my harrowing escape from the Communists who had taken over my country, already for twelve years then. I shall never forget that dream—or the events that came after it." She shut her eyes tightly for a moment.

The "charming Romanian" then consented to tell me the story of her life, a life rich and fascinating in its chiaroscuro of happiness and sorrow.

"Fortunately, I had been educated in England and spoke several languages," she said. "That proved a great help when I had to make a career for myself. That and my love of art were my salvation."

During her lifetime she had known wealth and privilege, then life-threatening danger and deprivation. She had known an unforgettable love, followed by an aching void. You felt that in her memories no chord of human emotion had been left unsounded.

What was her life like now? Her days were pleasantly filled with friends, family and her great passion for the arts. "And, of course, the season in Venice is always quite vigorous," her eyes brightened as she spoke these words. "There are parties every evening, and always so many exciting visitors in the city; a pity you aren't going to be here for the regatta..."

As she continued speaking, I noticed on the far wall an exquisite drawing of a young woman, hair swept back and a length of pearls encircling her slender throat.

184

She followed my gaze. "Yes, that is a portrait of me—oh, so many years ago. It's only a sketch, but it was by a very great artist—it all seems so long ago."

Before I left we laughed again over my mistaken assumption. What a huge joke we would have to tell our mutual friend. But then, as we said good-bye at the door, the "charming Romanian" held my arm and declared, "Wait, as a matter of fact, just lately, I've had the must unusual recurring dream; it's always the same. Let me tell you about it; maybe one of your 'psychics'—is that how they are called?—will know what it means."

Aha, I thought, perhaps this meeting was not, after all, merely a fortuitous mistake. Perhaps, during my hour with this wonderfully interesting and intelligent woman, I had made a convert to my cause.

Chapter 39

Paris, France: From a Darkened Basement to a Place Where All Times Intersect

I'm sometimes asked, "Suppose psychics could be persuaded to leave their brains to science, and suppose someone were to set up a foundation to receive and study these brains. Let's even assume that some major distinguishing features were discovered in these brains. Where would we be then?"

I can only say that this would certainly create the basis for a lot of interesting speculation (at the very least, it would be an argument for persuading science that *psi* does exist!). Then the questions could start off like this: What part of a psychic's brain "sees" or "senses" the future? What part of a psychic's brain is activated when the psychic reads someone's thoughts? Is the physical brain merely the conduit for the healing vibrations that have effected so many amazing cures?

We'll never begin to know the answers to these questions until we have a psychic's brain to study.

From Venice I flew on to Paris, the last stop in my journey, arriving in the French capital late on an October evening. The next day, I headed for the 20th *arrondisement*. I was anticipating an encounter of more than usual interest as I climbed up to the sixth-floor apartment on the Avenue Gambetta where I was soon to find Marie-Edith Marchante, *voyante*.

Marie-Edith was a small slender young woman who spoke in a soft, low-pitched voice. "I haven't used my English in 12 years," she quietly told me. "I have forgotten much." She said this as she was leading me down a narrow passageway to a small, sparsely furnished room where, she told me, "I give the readings."

Once we were seated, she removed the thick glasses she was wearing and revealed her huge gray eyes which had the diffuse unfocused gaze of a severely myopic person. "I'm very, very near-sighted," she told me, "but I think it may help me in my work. I have a different perspective, perhaps. I don't see the—outlines, is that the right word? I see the—"

"Extensions?" I suggested, recalling some psychic jargon.

"Yes, that's it; I see the 'extensions' of people."

With her dark hair falling to one side of her face, and her finely chiseled Gallic features heightened by the light from the open window, she could have been a model for a painting by Watteau. Surely, I thought, something mystifying to the reason must be going on behind those big gray eyes.

Marie-Edith immediately understood that I wasn't interested in being given a reading, but rather in the lives of those who were able to give readings, including hers. And, yes, she would tell me all about it.

She had been born in Toulon, on France's Mediterranean Cote d'Azur. "My childhood?" Marie-Edith repeated. "It was, I mean...I was always very sad, I was always dreaming. Not so much for any particular reason; I suppose it was just my temperament. I rarely studied in school at all, but I was always first in my age group, not just in my class, but for the entire city, and in every *métier*—every 'subject,' I think you say. I did not ever study, but I always knew the answers.

"As a child, I liked always to be alone. I didn't want anyone to get too close to me. I didn't find what others said very amusing."

It seemed that when she about the age of eight, Marie-Edith had fallen against an iron radiator and severely injured her head. After she had regained consciousness and been brought back from the hospital, she had found—certainly to her surprise!—that she could see the future.

"Friends of my parents would come to ask me questions," she explained. "My classmates would ask me questions. I began reading palms."

"What did your parents think?"

"Oh, they thought this was part of my being smart, like my knowing all the answers in school. No one on either side of my family was clairvoyant, so they didn't think of it in that way. My parents were very kind, very easy-going; they never worried much."

187

As she grew up Marie-Edith's reputation as a seer became more and more widely known, and an increasing number of clients came to her for readings. Ultimately, she moved to Paris, where she now had a large following.

"I am a clairvoyant and a clairaudient," she told me, "but I seldom make cures. Only two cures have I made, and those because the client insisted she wanted no one else but me. I prefer to give readings."

Marie-Edith said that, when giving a reading, she took on the physical sensations of the person she was 'seeing' clairvoyantly or 'hearing' clairaudiently. "If the person has a pain in the chest, I will have a pain in my chest. I will feel what the person is feeling. If you ask me about your friend and your friend has a headache, I will have a headache too. Do you understand?

"Because of this, the work is extremely draining for me. I find I lose a great amount of magnesium during a reading, and I must take regular magnesium supplements to offset this loss."

From the time of the blow to her head till her early twenties, Marie-Edith suffered every week from odd fainting spells lasting several minutes. "I would lose my consciousness—is that how you say it? After I was 20, it happened less and less. Now it happens only about once a year. It is not so serious, the doctors say."

"Do you think the blow to your head caused you to access some part of your brain not normally used?" I asked.

"Perhaps, but there was something else in my childhood that I have not told you about—something that I didn't know about myself until I was grown up."

Marie-Edith told me about a time when she was 24 and went to visit her parents. Since the last time she'd been to their apartment, several caged birds had been added, a gift from a friend. When she saw the birds beating their wings and flying about, Marie-Edith reacted in a surprising manner. She began to scream in inexplicable terror. Suspecting the reason for her fright, her mother told her for the first time a harrowing story from the past—a story about something that had happened to her when she was still too young consciously to remember it.

I listened as the bizarre tale unfolded. It seemed that Marie-Edith's paternal grandmother had been a member of the French nobility, but without the comfortable inheritance she had expected to receive. Her father had squandered the entire family fortune, leaving his daughter angry, disappointed, and desperately poor.

"It's quite hard to be titled and to be left with no lands and no money," Marie-Edith stated in her grandmother's defense.

Resentment had turned to bitterness, and bitterness had turned to madness. Marie-Edith's parents had been unaware of the state of mental deterioration of her grandmother and had left their child, less than two years old, in her care.

Every day of the six months of Marie-Edith's visit, the old woman had placed the child in a windowless basement room and left her there all alone for several hours in total darkness. The cellar was filled with noisy barnyard fowl and flapping bats that flew about and pecked at the frightened child who could only cry out in helpless anguish.

"How unbelievably cruel!" I exclaimed.

"Yes, very cruel. My grandmother had really gone quite mad."

When Marie-Edith's parents returned for their child and learned to their horror what had taken place, all they could do was hope that time would erase the effects of what had happened.

"Now, I will tell you something very interesting," Marie-Edith continued. "I read once that in ancient Egypt there was a strange practice designed to made a person more—'spiritual,' is that the word? I'm not really sure that is the word, but something like it."

As Marie-Edith remembered it, candidates for 'spiritual' elevation were forced to walk alone through a long tunnel to the walls of which were chained ferocious beasts. In the darkness, the candidates had no way of knowing that the beasts were chained; hearing the growls and roars, they feared for their lives at every step.

"It was a very important 'spiritual' experience for the ancient Egyptians, I believe," Marie-Edith told me. "Perhaps what happened to me was a bit like that."

I could offer no opinion as to just what such an ordeal might have done for the ancient Egyptians—maybe it did cause them to shift into higher gear—but I was able to assure Marie-Edith that, given the tender age at which she'd been forced to suffer her ordeal, she was fortunate she hadn't been traumatized for life! I wondered to myself too if those days of terror in the darkness might not account for her extreme myopia.

Marie-Edith told me she'd always been vitally interested in anthropology, and studied the subject in great depth. She frankly preferred books to people: "I am very reserved and easily bored by most conversations," she confessed. This French *voyante* had written a book on Aztec symbolism that was just then being edited for publication. "I read everything I can find about the Aztec people," she told me. "I have a passion for all things of that civilization."

Marie-Edith had been brought up as a Catholic, but now she adhered to no formal religious faith. "Though, of course, I believe in God," she was quick to add.

"I also believe in reincarnation, but I do not think it is like most people imagine it to be. And certainly most people have a very wrong notion of time! The past, the present, and the future all exist together, but in different dimensions—and what it is important to remember is that at a particular moment, in a particular place, you can find past and future intersecting." Marie-Edith placed the edge of one hand on the edge of the other, forming a cross. "Do you understand what I'm saying?"

Frantically trying to keep up, I asked her to give me from her own personal experience an example of this intersecting of times.

"Well, yes," she said slowly. "You will find it quite odd, but I'll tell you." She leaned forward, half-closing her eyes as she began:

"Once, I was having tea with a young man and some friends in an outdoor café, when all of a sudden, from behind the house across the street, I saw, as if I were seeing *through* the house, a huge, solid, white column rising up from the earth toward the sky. The column seemed to be magnetic—do you say it like that?—and I was drawn to it, my mind, my soul, or however you want to call it, and then my body as well.

"I went through the front of the house, then through two of its walls, and then into the column itself. Yet I knew I was still chatting and having tea with my friends. I was in two places at once! While I was inside the column, I met many people—from the past, the present, the future—and I was able to verify this in the case of two of the people, one in the present and one in the future."

I listened in amazement as Marie-Edith told me this story. I urged her to continue.

"The experience of someone in the *present* I could verify immediately, because I asked him his name. Since at the same time I was seated having tea, the answer he gave me passed in an arc over my head, accompanied, or so it seemed, by music. When I spoke the person's name aloud, the young man I was with in the café looked startled; it was the name of a friend of his who lived a long way off. Three days later, to his surprise, the friend appeared at his door!

"The other person in the column whom I was eventually able to identify was a woman from the future. After we had talked for a while, she invited me to her house in the country, giving me the address of a place quite remote from Paris. I made a mental note of that address. Many months later, a client who knew I was writing a book asked me if I'd like to use her country house in a distant region of France, where I would be able to work in undisturbed quiet. She gave me the key and the address. The address, in a lonely area with very few roads, turned out to be the house next door to the house of the woman in the column."

"What do you make of all this?" I asked, bewildered and fascinated.

"I really don't know," Marie-Edith confessed, "but I believe the position of the column, the spot from which it arose, must have been where magnetic lines cross on the earth—something to do with the intersection of times, I believe." Her eyes rested on a point above my head even as they retained their diffused gaze. She seemed completely absorbed in her thoughts.

"That is quite a story, no?" she said, lowering her eyes.

When I asked her about the future in general, Marie-Edith told me she was not too greatly discouraged. "Women will continue to gain independence, and that is good. There won't be total devastation, but the next 20 years will be hard—there will be economic and social upheaval. Then, after 20, maybe 30 more years, there will be a great spiritual awakening. What will bring this about? I think some sort of discovery in outer space...yes, I think it will have to do with our exploration of space."

The big gray eyes glanced anxiously at her watch.

"I've kept you too long," I said. "Do forgive me."

"No, no," she quickly replied, "it's just that my family is coming for lunch, and I must prepare."

I tried not to hear this final statement. I wanted to remember Marie-Edith in her white column, standing at some magnetic crossroads of the earth. I certainly didn't want to remember her in the kitchen!

As I journeyed back through Paris, I thought of Marie-Edith's grandmother, of that poor woman's wasted life, of her being driven to madness by the meanness of shattered expectations. I was reminded of an aging beauty I'd known of in Argentina, who'd once been courted by the cousin of a European monarch. For whatever reason, that romance had not culminated in marriage—and the Argentinian beauty had been in a bad mood ever since. She was well into her eighties now, and for more than 50 years her once-classic features had been set in a petulant frown. A lifetime of grumpiness seemed a high price to pay for a few bittersweet memories and a handful of crested souvenirs. I decided that there was a lot to be said for a belief in reincarnation, if such a belief could save us from taking our individual lives too seriously.

I remained in Paris for several days, happy for the chance to catch up with old friends; then, I booked an early flight back to America. I wondered if there would be a letter from Barrie at the internist's. Might Barrie be willing to submit to exploratory tests? Might his doctor have decided that such tests were potentially harmful? That they could interfere, perhaps, with his unique digestive processes?

I headed back to Atlanta, filled with anxiety and hope.

Chapter 40

Atlanta, Georgia, and London, England: Barrie Tries to Help Us All

During my long flight across the Atlantic I reflected on the many things I had seen and heard in the past few months. I wondered if the scrambling of energy patterns involved in spoon bending could be the same process as the one that turns caterpillars into butterflies. I wondered if a medium's so-called 'control' could be merely the creation of a persona to fill an unrecognized need; having received little validation in their childhoods, mediums might be able to accept their own insights *only* if they could believe those insights came from a revered source outside themselves. Could the control (the Indian king, the deceased Prime Minister, the spirit doctors, and so on) be only an unconscious invention of the medium, triggered unawares by a lack of "sense of self?"

If this were so, what about the circle on Biki's shoulder?

I remembered youthful Karima Tatum shuffling her colorful Tarot cards in the warm Hawaiian sunlight and telling me, "I only use these cards to read the qualities within persons that could have an impact on their futures. People's fates should be left in their own hands." If, as Ouspensky reminds us, any given lifetime is the fulfillment of only one of myriad possibilities, then it seemed to me we had a large measure of control over which possibility would be fulfilled.

I thought about Nancy Wodehouse and her admonition to watch our thoughts: "Thoughts, we know, are energy, and energy is a cause, and a cause will inevitably have an effect..."

When I finally arrived home, a letter from Barrie indeed awaited me. I was pleased to find out that my letter from Delhi had reached him. And I was happy about his answer:

"I was delighted to receive your letter and to hear about your interesting trip to the Far East. Yes, it was interesting what Ramesh Paramahamsa said. I am sure mind power is involved in this. Dur-

ing the readings, a lot of different doctors came through who were talking to me while Gwen was in trance. Gwen's mind could have affected my mind, who knows; but the results have been astonishing. I think your idea of having the tests in London is best, and I will make some inquiries."

A few mornings later, Barrie telephoned me to say he'd already talked with a well-known gastroenterologist who'd ordered certain x-rays and screening studies. "He says I belong in the *Guinness Book of Records*," Barrie laughingly reported as he described the visit. "I have an appointment at the end of the month with a consulting radiologist who will take the x-rays."

"Now, listen, Barrie," I said, feeling anxious again, "don't have any x-rays or any tests if you have *any* misgivings whatsoever."

"On the contrary," he replied, "I'm looking forward to this. Perhaps, if we find out what's going on inside me, the knowledge can be used to help others. It will be interesting in any event."

"I'll be there at the end of the month," I told him.

Then I called Gwennie, who was also relieved: "I'm glad Barrie will be seeing a doctor in London rather than making a trip to some 'foreign country.' Don't think they'll find anything though," she concluded, in her characteristically abrupt manner.

Chapter 41

New Orleans, Louisiana: Did an Act of Selfless Love Cause a Blind Eye to See Again?

Less than a week had gone by since I'd gotten back to Atlanta when I learned of another strange and unexplained healing, one that had greatly troubled the medical community of New Orleans. The circumstances under which this healing took place, and the time frame involved, made it a particularly intriguing one. I was determined to track down the principals in hopes of learning more.

It seemed that, in 1985, a young Louisiana woman named Caroline Henry had been scheduled to undergo surgery for the removal of a small brain tumor. To comply with the law, Caroline Henry had been made to sign an "informed consent" after she'd been told she could possibly lose the sight of one or both her eyes.

"I was so scared, so scared," Caroline recalled with a shudder as we talked.

"I'd had my right eye operated on two years before to reattach a detached retina. I remembered this as a bad experience, and my present problem was, of course, a much more serious one. I was just plain terrified."

On the appointed day, Caroline's brain tumor was successfully removed with no complications whatsoever. Nevertheless, for some unaccountable reason, Caroline Henry's right eye, the one that had undergone the previous trauma, was now totally blind.

A number of years passed, during which a wonderful new ophthalmic tool was developed: laser sculpturing of the cornea to correct acute near-sightedness. This was a highly delicate procedure, and a long period of training and practice was required before a surgeon could feel competent to perform it on a patient. I'd been told that the surgeon-in-training began by working on frozen cow eyes, then went on to blind guinea pig eyes, then on up the scale to the higher apes. The final training procedure was done on the blind eye of a human being.

195

Caroline's mother persuaded Caroline to offer her blind eye for this final, ultimate training stage. "Think of it as an experiment," she told her daughter. "Think how much you'll be helping someone else have better vision."

Though she was reluctant to undergo surgery again, Caroline finally agreed. "I told my mother, 'All right, I'll do it, if it can really help someone else see better.'"

I asked Caroline: "When the day arrived, what did you think? What were you feeling?" I could imagine how difficult this must have been for her.

She answered, "I was scared—just plain scared! I was able to control my fears by thinking: 'This is going to help someone; this is going to help someone *see* better...'"

When the bandages were removed from her eye three days after the operation, Caroline was in great pain. But after a short time, the pain subsided, and she was able to take up her life again, happy in the knowledge that her blind eye had at least contributed to improving someone else's sight.

About eight weeks after the practice surgery, Caroline was at a children's party with her small son. "Things sort of got out of control," she told me, laughing as she described the scene. "Finally, some teacakes began to be thrown about, and one hit me squarely in the face. I remember raising my hands quickly to protect my eyes.

"After washing off the crumbs, I splashed cold water on my face. When I looked up—I could see perfectly out of both eyes! I quickly covered my left eye. I couldn't believe it! After six years of total blindness, the vision in my right eye was clear and perfect.

"I rushed back to the doctor's office shouting, 'I can see, I can see!' The doctor was completely shocked. She covered my left eye, then put up eye charts with letters, then eye charts with colors—anything and everything to test my vision. I could see perfectly out of my right eye! There was no way to explain it. It was like some sort of miracle."

Astonished and moved by Caroline's story, I subsequently talked to the ophthalmic surgeon herself, who corroborated the medical facts of the story. The surgeon finished by quietly saying, "We really don't have any explanation for the restoration of Caroline Henry's sight."

As I listened to the account of this happy miracle, I suddenly remembered the words of Nancy Wodehouse, spoken to me in Italy a few years before, about the power of a totally unselfish act. Perhaps, I thought, *just perhaps*, the explanation lay therein: in the power set in motion, in the energy released, by Caroline's willingness to go beneath the surgeon's knife in the hope of helping others.

Chapter 42

Atlanta, Georgia:
A Nationally Recognized Civic Volunteer Discovers
the Mixed Blessing of Premonitions

By now, I should have been completely inured to the unexpected. But I was still unprepared for a surprising "find" within my own neighborhood: a remarkable young woman to whom flattering adjectives such as "intelligent," "articulate," and "charming" were routinely applied, who had known much worldly success—and who, unbeknownst to almost everyone, possessed the powerful gift of 'psychic illumination.'

This was a woman whom I'd long admired and who appeared to enjoy an unusually happy, active and successful life. Other epithets regularly applied to her were "efficient" and "a born leader." She had chaired boards on the city, state, and national level. At one time, she had been head of all art museum volunteers throughout the United States and Canada. She had been honored by a State House of Representatives resolution. While in her thirties, she had been selected one of the "Ten Outstanding Young Women in America." She had taken these offices and accolades blithely in stride, never ceasing to build upon them. Charitable organizations, conservation groups, education forums—all continually sought her strong leadership and no-nonsense expertise.

It was quite by accident that I learned that the "something else" that no one would ever have suspected of this highly capable person—the something she hardly ever mentioned herself—was her random experiencing of psychic illuminations of startling accuracy.

The woman's name was Elizabeth Hale Barnett. She had been born in Tennessee and had grown up in Delaware. Beth was the third of five children of adoring parents, and she had only the happiest memories of her early years.

"When did you first realize that you were psychic?" I asked, still in a state of shock at having learned that Beth Barnett, civic

leader, campaign organizer and board chairman, also had the gift
of *psi*.

"I suppose I realized when I was quite young that I 'knew' things
without understanding how I knew them," she told me. "I think my
mother was aware of this, though we seldom spoke of it." Beth
laughed as she remembered, "At school, I never really understood
mathematics. I could always come up with the correct answer, yet
be totally unable to explain by what process I had reached it. My
bewildered teachers must have found me a frustrating student.

"But in some ways, the gift of *psi* can be quite frightening. Some
of my own premonitions have been of a highly distressing nature.
For example, a few years ago, as I drove to my various appointments, I would 'see' before my eyes a bridge and an embankment.
This vision continued for several days—always of a bridge and an
embankment. I told my husband about this recurring vision and
my feeling of foreboding. He urged me to drive very carefully,
asking me if the vision had anything to do with me. 'No,' I told
him, 'It's someone else, not me.'

"Suddenly the feeling ceased. That same afternoon, the telephone rang. 'That's it!' I exclaimed to myself. I knew the call
would reveal the explanation for my vision.

"The call brought the shattering news that one of my friends
had gone off a bridge over an embankment and been killed.

"Another such premonition ended equally tragically. Once,
while shopping at a market on the outskirts of the city, I suddenly
had a strange, uneasy feeling, which gradually grew into a state of
near-panic. I became terrifyingly certain of imminent danger threatening someone close to me. I rushed home and telephoned my
husband and our two sons. All three were safe and well, but the
depressing sensation continued. Several hours later, it ended. And
then a call came: My little nephew, just home from summer camp
that morning, had been killed by a deranged neighbor!

"Such insights obviously travel on highly emotional energy
bands, but I don't understand them any more than you do."

I quickly asked her: "What are the actual physical sensations
accompanying such visions?"

She answered, "Before they come, I have a sort of dark, unclear sense of something 'impending,' like a dark cloud. Along with that, I have a feeling of indescribable heaviness, a great weariness.

"Mercifully, the gift doesn't always manifest itself in such a negative way. In a discussion or an argument sometimes, I can simultaneously participate and 'observe'—an enormous advantage, as you can well imagine. I can be inside the action and watching it at the same time. I also seem to have total auditory recall. Just as those who have photographic memories can actually picture whole pages of a newspaper, I can accurately remember verbatim pieces of dialogue and whole conversations.

"When I enter a room full of people, I can immediately sense positive or negative vibrations. I'm able to pick up on all sorts of non-verbal signals. It's a gift for which I'm very grateful. I only wish the premonitions of impending tragedy were more specific so that I could somehow intercede. One of my sons seems to be in a kind of mental affinity with me. He 'knows' when I am experiencing this feeling of foreboding, and he telephones me immediately."

With her clear blue eyes, flashing smile and boundless energy, Beth looked as she spoke the epitome of radiant health. When I mentioned this, she was quick to remark that some years earlier she had been forced to undergo a series of painful operations.

"Maybe the suffering served to make me more sensitive," she remarked. "Who can say? I only know that I have always had such an enormous zest for life. I want it for myself and for others, in abundance. I think my sufferings gave me a sixth sense regarding people's needs. Even speaking before an audience in a room filled with strangers, I seem able to pick up on what each one has come there to hear. I look upon the psychic gift, however randomly it may occur, as a skill, a talent, a tool, which can improve the quality of a person's performance and perhaps even protect and guide."

"What do you think will be the attitude in the future towards *psi*?" I asked. "Will it ever gain the respect it deserves?"

"Let's hope so!" Beth answered emphatically. "It's an awesome resource that we can't afford to ignore. To those who see it as a threat, or think of it as potentially dangerous, I can only say that if we don't risk, we don't live!"

As I left Beth's quiet garden with its gracefully flowering shrubs and carefully clipped borders, I remembered the cryptic words of the Sufi Firoz, who said: "If you can find anything in this life which is without any danger of abuse and lacks risk, tell me, and I shall spend all my time in concentration on it."

Beth Barnett was a shining example of the way in which even a touch of the psychic gift, when found in a stable personality, can enhance that person's life.

Chapter 43

New York, N.Y.: A Modern-Day Ariadne Seeks to Lead Us Out of the Contemporary Labyrinth

M aria Papapetrous was born on the island of Crete, two-and-a-half miles from the ancient palace at Knossos. She lived there till age 20, when she moved to the U.S. and New York City.

You sensed a tremendous strength in this handsome woman. I liked to imagine that in her youth Maria had resembled the brave Ariadne of Greek legend, who helped Theseus slay the dreaded Minotaur and escaped with him from the imprisoning labyrinth on Crete. Unlike Ariadne's father, however, Maria's father was not a mythical "King of Crete," but instead a respected member of the diplomatic service who had made certain, before he brought them to America, that his children learned English, attended the Greek Orthodox Church, and received the finest education Crete could offer.

Maria recalled to me that whenever as a very young child she'd heard English spoken, it had sounded somehow "familiar," and she'd always "known" America would be her home one day.

Her first experience of the paranormal took place when an older cousin gave her a wrist watch without explaining how it worked. When the watch stopped working Maria was frantic, fearing she had done something wrong and having no idea how to start it up again. In a dream that night, she saw a man pull the stem out of the watch, move the hands, then turn the stem back and forth until the watch started ticking again. When the child awoke she tried this herself; to her delight, the dream instructions proved correct. From that moment on, Maria was convinced of the power of the subconscious.

"The answers are there. The answers are within us," she told me. "We must learn how to tap into them in our waking state."

After she arrived in America, Maria studied psychology and later cosmetology. She decided to open a hairdressing studio, and

202

found that when she touched a client's head to arrange her hair, she could pick up information about the person's past and future. This shouldn't have been surprising, since two of Maria's aunts were well-known in Greece for their gift of prophesying. Realizing that she, too, had this remarkable talent, Maria began to give readings. "The impressions are flashed on the screen of my mind," she explained. "That is the best way I can describe it, and sometimes the visions are in color and sometimes in black and white."

"Is there a physical out-picturing at this time?" I asked.

"Oh, yes," she told me. "I can feel it in my whole body if the client is suffering from a problem, but if things are going well with him I feel fine. When I give a reading, I close my eyes and mentally 'place a light' around the person and around myself, and then I silently pray that the information I give will be beneficial to all, that it will be specific and direct and true, and that it will come from the God-source and flow effortlessly through me.

"Luckily, when I finish my day's work I know how to 'detach.' Then I go out with my friends and enjoy life like anyone else. I read a great deal, and I like to write.

"I also spend time in meditative communication with my son who died at the age of 16. He was such a bright child, with an I.Q. of 168. That fine mind lives on. He once 'communicated' to me that he was with Lord Nelson on the water and playing with the lions. I thought to myself that this made no sense: There are no lions at sea.

"Shortly afterward, I was summoned to London to work in a film. My first stop was at Trafalgar Square—and there stood the stature of Nelson, above a water fountain supporting three massive sculptured lions."

For several years, Maria lived on the West Coast and was a film consultant at Paramount Studios. While out in California she was asked to take part in a study of psychics being conducted at U.C.L.A. by Dr. Jan Berlin. At the conclusion of the study, Dr. Berlin rated Maria the most gifted of all the participants. Thereafter, whenever the police—or any other persons—sought the help of a psychic, it was to Maria that the University referred them.

Maria Papapetrous insisted to me that everyone had a talent like hers to some degree, adding, "My goal is to be instrumental in removing the cloak of 'exclusivity' from clairvoyance. I assure you that it can be developed to some degree by everyone. It *must* be developed, for it elevates the human spirit. It indeed represents the direction of our evolution."

Chapter 44

London, England: Epitaph for a Great Healer: "God Is the Source of the Messages I Hear"

At the end of the month I returned to London. I found Barrie even more hopeful that something might be learned from his condition that could enhance the lives of others.

It was with high hearts that the two of us set out for Harley Street.

Barrie's doctor presented us with a long and technical review of Barrie's early medical records and the doctor's own recent findings. Then he stated his conclusions simply and succinctly:

"The case, to my knowledge, is totally unique. There is nothing in my experience I can relate it to. Here is a man in excellent health, exhibiting none of the toxicity evident before this amazing change took place in his metabolism. I really don't know how the toxic wastes have been disposed of for these past 17 years, and I think it would be most unwise to take him apart to try to find out. The digestive processes he now enjoys might be disturbed." As we left the office, the doctor gave Barrie a pat on the shoulder and said: "You're in great shape. Just be thankful!"

I wasn't too surprised, but I was keenly disappointed, particularly for Barrie's sake. He had been so hopeful that at some future time his condition might be replicated in others. But, as we drove away from the doctor's office, we both sadly agreed it was highly unlikely that what had happened to him would ever be repeated. Gwennie's spirit doctors had told her in trance that, in attempting to heal Barrie, they had wanted to "try an experiment." Gwennie herself doubted she would ever achieve the same results again.

(Incidentally, the well-known Harley Street physician asked that his name not be used. Here was yet another example of a scientist's reluctance to be associated with the inexplicable.)

Perhaps Barrie will one day leave his body to science; perhaps, then, something can be learned—or perhaps nothing. Perhaps Gwennie

Scott will one day leave her brain for study—though when I once suggested it she replied, "What for?" and dismissed the subject.

Barrie seemed to think that in his case another dimension was involved, one of which we have no understanding (so had pronounced Odelon; see Chapter 21); Barrie believed the metabolic process took place there, with results that were reflected in his body. "It looks as though we can only know the results, never the process," he remarked to me, "and that the workings of Gwennie's incredible mind will likely remain a mystery forever."

The question then arises: Is such psychic clairaudience—hearing the messages of spirit guides—a part of the same gift that enables a psychic to retrieve lost objects? Does the ability to look into a glass of water or a crystal ball and 'see' a future event spring from the same source that enables some to touch an object and sense its history, as is the case with the psychometrist? Just as intellectual endowment is manifested in a variety of ways, are diverse paranormal abilities simply different facets of a single gift?

My search for the psychically talented could have gone on for years. But I knew that in the end I would have little more knowledge about the roots of this fascinating phenomenon than I did when I started out. One person's guess is as good as another's. Until science is willing to take a serious look at the paranormal, we can only wait and wonder.

I realized, too, that I would have needed to interview perhaps thousands of psychics in order to establish a sufficiently large sampling from which to even generalize. I am aware that what I have produced here is a mere random sampling, only a handful of interviews with women alleged to be psychic. The commonalities that I so often found among them—early head injury, severe childhood illness, emotional trauma, parents or other relatives with the same gift, physical sensations preceding episodes, highly sensitive natures—all of these can easily be written off as purely coincidental and merely anecdotal. Even those manifestations of their gifts that I personally experienced—healings, bolts of energy, messages—can perhaps be explained by the power of suggestion, or by a talent which we all share to some extent: simple self-deception.

Be that as it may. Can anyone explain the change in Barrie Stonehill on any other basis than what we loosely call the "metaphysical?" Can anyone deny that the mind of Gwennie Scott somehow played a catalytic role in the healing—was, perhaps, the conduit?

We might also wonder whether it was simply by chance that all the women I happened to interview appeared to be using the psychic gift positively. I firmly believe that it was *not* by chance. I believe, rather, that the possession of the gift elevates those who possess it. The "connectedness of all things," which all psychics seem to sense, must surely influence their attitude toward the earth and toward their fellow human beings. If this spiritually neutral gift is found in a person of even marginal morality, then its effect cannot help but be uplifting.

Gwennie and I had a final visit together. "I'm nearing 85," she told me with a sigh, "and getting very, very tired. I'm not taking any new patients any more. I still treat a few old ones whom I've taken care of in the past, but my strength is giving out, my dear. I guess I'm looking forward now to emigrating to my natural home."

We talked for a while about her remarkable gift. "Oh, please don't praise me," she protested, as she had so often done in the past. Once again she stressed the necessity for compassion and deep humility in the practice of healing. "There can be no pride attached," she insisted to me. "The creator, God, the source of all life—that is the source of the messages I hear. I am only a conduit. I merely use the power of my mind to channel this healing love.

"They talk about the Big Bang," she said with a laugh, "the Big Bang that brought the universe into being. Who, what spirit, what energy, do they think caused this 'Big Bang?' And who created that which went 'bang?' Who created the void into which a million galaxies could endlessly expand? There's got to be a cause. There's got to be a source.

"Oh, yes; and there's got to be a reason. We are all here to learn lessons, you know, and we'll keep coming back until we've learned them. Man's ultimate goal, the Holy Grail he's reaching for, is union with the source, with God. Then man will become a part of creation itself." Gwennie's eyes took on that distant look.

207

The years seemed to melt away from her features. For a moment, she looked almost young.

"It's late," she said brusquely, holding onto her chair as she heaved herself up from the table. "You'll miss your train back into town. We can't just sit here talking all day as though we had nothing better to do!"

She and the deaf cat followed me out the door and along to the gate; she was still waving to me as I turned the corner.

A few months later, Barrie telephoned to say that Gwennie had died. "She changed my entire life, you know," he told me quietly.

"Yes," I answered, "and in a way, she's also changed mine."

Chapter 45

Newark, New Jersey: Death and the Burdens of Female Prophetic Power

When I decided to put my findings together in a book, several people insisted there could not be a *bona fide* book on female psychics which didn't include Laura Mangeiameli.

Laura Mangeiameli's was a well-known name in psychic circles. She had been "active in this field," as she put it, for over 40 years. Laura was a great friend of the "sleeping prophet," Edgar Cayce, and had worked closely with him on several occasions. Her own psychic predictions were carefully validated, with reams of letters and affidavits attesting to their authenticity.

The widow of an Italian nuclear engineer, Laura Mangeiameli lived alone in a retirement complex some fifty miles south of Newark, New Jersey. She told me over the telephone that she was getting old, and suffered from Parkinson's Disease. But she kindly agreed to see me if I would come up to New Jersey. We made an appointment for the following week.

Once I'd found the correct exit off the New Jersey Turnpike, the directions to her house were easy to follow. I arrived at Laura's door a few minutes early.

I'd known from her voice that Laura Mangeiameli was English, and that by her own admission she was no longer young and not in the best of health. But I was totally unprepared for those eyes. I had never seen eyes of such an intense blue. They appeared to have no pupils at all, and, through that long afternoon that we talked and laughed, they almost never faltered in their steady penetrating gaze.

Laura gave every indication of being an extremely happy person and, despite her illness, totally comfortable with her life and how she was using it. "Parkinson's has slowed me down somewhat," she told me with a sigh, "but I don't think it has affected my psychic ability, and I am very thankful for that."

Though she was a descendant of two very illustrious British families, Laura offhandedly remarked that her generation and her particular branch of those families had little money. "But we've never felt it mattered very much," she confided. "We've been extremely close and happy. And what you've never known personally, you don't miss."

When she was nine years old, Laura had suffered a severely traumatic accident which left one of her legs badly injured. She'd been forced to leave school and remain at home for many months to recuperate. During that period, confined to her bed and often alone, Laura had begun to hear people talking in the empty room. Strange visions began to flash vividly before her eyes. These occurrences took place completely at random; but, since she assumed others were having similar experiences, Laura was never frightened by them.

Surprisingly, her parents, particularly her mother, never questioned the child nor discouraged her when she talked about these strange and random happenings. Laura was to learn later that in each generation of the two families from which she was descended, the psychic gift had always appeared in one form or another.

I asked her if the gift had appeared in the next generation—in her own children.

"Yes," she replied, "one son has it to a degree, and I have a five-year-old granddaughter who is very psychic. Some of my psychic ancestors suffered gravely from persecution. People fear what they can't understand, I suppose. Well, at least we aren't burned as witches anymore," she laughed, "and even some scientists are becoming grudgingly interested in *psi*. My own late husband was a scientist, and...with so many of my own predictions coming true, he had no choice but to believe.

"I believe the psychic gift is to be used to help others, but we have to truly love our fellow humans in order to be able to help them. I've been counseling, advising and giving readings for forty years. I don't do any healing; I don't want to run afoul of the medical community." Laura laughed again, "But I can tell you there are some truly wonderful psychic healers in this world."

210

"If a person comes to you for a reading," I asked, "what is the procedure?"

"I sit very quietly. Then I sort of tune in, and 'see' and 'hear.' While this is happening, I have a strange sensation in the region of my solar plexus. I can't explain it, but it's a very real sensation.

"I feel that psychics must guard against becoming too popular—is that the word? Too worldly. The gift must not be—how shall I say it?—too exploited. Greed can be very detrimental. And don't forget, it's a gift; it's not something one can learn. I do think, though, that in the human brain there is always this potential, and it is we who are psychic who have somehow accessed it. If we don't try to use the gift for selfish purposes, I believe that, as it is more and more developed, mankind will become increasingly spiritually elevated—just as increased morality usually accompanies intellectual growth."

I concurred, recalling the maxim of French cynic La Rochefoucauld that "The more rational we become, the more we blush at our motives and inclinations."

"In any event," concluded Laura, "I believe we're continuing to evolve."

I wanted to ask her, "Don't you think that what you and other psychics are experiencing may represent the first feeble steps toward the full-blown psychic powers which someday all mankind will enjoy?" But no one likes the word "feeble," and so I hesitated.

As if reading my thoughts, Laura added with an enigmatic smile, "Oh, yes, my dear, I think we're in the vanguard—and I do think scientists are beginning to be, well, at least curious, if not entirely receptive." Then she brought out stacks of letters confirming predictions she had made; many of them bore impressive signatures.

"I remember vividly one instance of my clairvoyance that involved great sadness," Laura told me. "It concerned a wonderful family I loved very much."

She sat back in her deep armchair, and for once let her gaze slip away from me as she contemplated that sad experience.

"It was during the war in Vietnam," Laura Mangeiameli began slowly, "and one of this family's sons, Mike Mitchell, named for his uncle Mike Charles, was in the thick of the fighting near Da Nang. It was a tense time for the family, and they often came to me for comfort and guidance. I remember so well that beautiful April day when the family came for one of their visits. As she was leaving, the mother asked me, 'Do you have a message from Mike? He's safe, isn't he?'

"'Yes, he's safe,' I answered. But just after I said this, I had a vision of an explosion.

"I spent many sleepless nights after that visit worrying because I hadn't told them what I'd seen. I prayed for forgiveness and hoped the vision would go away. But whenever I turned into 'spirit'—you understand what I mean by that—I saw the same picture.

"I constantly sent out my love to little Mike, and as I did so Mike's mind and my mind became one. Can you understand that? Whenever his mother received a letter from him, I knew when it came; I knew what it contained; I knew how he felt. And always, I kept praying that the picture of the explosion was wrong.

"Some three weeks later, when I returned home from a trip, I had a terrific headache and asked my husband to answer the telephone if it rang. He sensed that I disliked answering the telephone at all now, for fear "that call" would come. Suddenly the phone did ring. The family wanted to come and see me the next day. Nothing was said, no information was given—just that they *had* to see me.

"I awaited our appointment anxiously. When the family came, I dared to ask them, 'How is young Mike?' Their reply was, 'He's fine. He telephoned over the weekend.' I felt a deep sense of relief, and I thanked God. Then we sat down, and I was told they all had a single question which they hoped I could answer.

"Just as I always do, I sat with my cross in one hand and an article of theirs in the other—in this case, a broken window handle. As I was attuning myself to 'spirit,' I heard a voice saying, 'I'm Mike.' This was most upsetting to me, and I mentally asked for a clearer explanation while responding to the voice I was hearing.

"Then I heard the voice say, 'I'm Mike Charles.' It was the uncle! At this point, I knew I couldn't run away from the vision.

The family had to be told of my repeated picture of an explosion—and also that Mike Charles was now 'in spirit,' as we say when someone has passed over.

"What I didn't know then—though the family did—was that four days earlier, there had indeed been an explosion, aboard an oil tanker off Staten Island. Mike Charles had been on that oil tanker. Though his wife had been told he'd been listed as "missing," she was clinging to the belief that he was still alive.

"Whether Mike Charles was alive was, of course, the question that the family had come here to ask me.

"But alas, the voice talked on about the children Mike Charles had left behind, about the fact that his body would not be found for five weeks, about his wearing a Masonic ring on his finger. The voice gave instructions as to what should be done in his home, including the admonition that his daughter should not delay her marriage because of her father's death.

"Mike Charles's sister was sitting next to me—and the voice repeated the last words Mike had said to her before he boarded the ill-fated tanker. The sister was stunned. The voice expressed his concern for his brother, Richard, who had just been involved in an accident. He said he had been there with him all the time and that Richard should have 'sensed' his presence during the rescue. He even explained that the window handle I was holding was the one he had taken off a window to repair.

"The evidence that this was Mike was overwhelming.

"After the family left I thought to myself: 'So that is the explosion I saw. At least, little Mike is safe.' But the vision wouldn't go away. It kept reoccurring. I wondered if there could be yet another explosion which would affect the lives of this dear family.

"One day, little Mike told me via telepathy that he had written to his mother telling her he was going to re-enlist. When next his mother came to see me, the letter was in her purse; she had just received it. I immediately sensed danger. The old panic overtook me once again. Little Mike's mother asked me to write him and ask him to change his mind; maybe, she said, he would do it for me. I told her not to think that little Mike had forgotten her Mother's

Day flowers—they would arrive late—but, oddly enough, as I spoke I saw two uniforms around them which I could not understand.

"I did write to little Mike, begging him to forget about re-enlisting and come home. He replied with a very lovely letter. I wish you could have seen it. That letter was a wonderful tribute to every mother's son who has fought in the service of his country."

Her intense blue eyes closed now as she continued: "Six days later, little Mike, too, was taken—by an explosion. His little bouquet of flowers arrived late, just as I had 'seen,' and at the same time there were two uniformed soldiers—two—who came to notify his mother of his passing. Little Mike continued to communicate with me clearly, even to the smallest details, which offered strong evidence to his family that their loved ones lived on, and that there is communication from beyond the grave. I'm proud to remember that I was an instrument that could help them."

This extraordinary demonstration by Laura Mangeiameli raises many questions. Whenever Laura had concentrated on her brave young friend fighting in Vietnam, she had 'seen' an explosion. Was the vision telling her the boy was destined to be killed by an explosion? Or was the vision given to her so she might try to persuade him—as indeed she tried—not to re-enlist? If young Mike had heeded her plea to come home, would he then have been spared?

What is involved here is the age-old question of predestination. Is the future "out there," in all its entirety, simply waiting for our arrival? And, if this is so, to what extent can we alter the script?

P.D. Ouspensky speculated that there are many "futures" out there, somehow perpendicular to our linear conception of time. If that is true, then it must be we who, by our thoughts and actions, decide which "future" will be realized in our consciousness.

A more immediate question is: What part of Laura Mangeiameli's brain was capable of 'seeing' an explosion that had yet to take place and could or would impact violently on the life of someone close to her? Again, a high degree of emotional content seems to be an important factor here. Will all of us one day be capable of accessing that part of our own brain? Or does Laura Mangeiameli's brain in some way differ anatomically from ours?

Chapter 46

In Conclusion: An Anthropologist, a Psychiatrist, a Physician and a Theologian Speak Out

Some years ago, at a conference on brain research, I heard the celebrated doctor who performed the autopsy on a part of Einstein's brain deliver a spell-binding lecture. While showing slides of her findings, she pointed out the plethora of glia-cells in Einstein's brain, speculating that these represented a far greater number than in the normal brain.

She had hardly completed her lecture before a number of scientists leapt to their feet. "How can you say 'more than in a normal brain?'" was basically their question. "We haven't had enough brains to study in order to form a proper control, so how can we say how many glia-cells will be found in a normal brain?"

This verbal battle impressed me enormously. If, one day, scientists are able to definitively describe a "normal brain," how will the brain of the psychic differ from this, if at all—and how will we be able to find out? Perhaps non-invasive studies (for example, PET and MRI scans) should be made of the brains of recognized psychics during their lifetimes, and these psychics should be urged to will their brains to science for further study after death.

Surely the first step ought to be the identification of those genuinely gifted in the psychic sense. In order for there to be impartial testing, a jury would have to contain an equal number of people who recognize the existence of *psi* and people who are skeptical.

All true psychics affirm that the gift—at best fragile, even unstable—is affected by the thoughts of those around them. They know that, even for the most gifted "sensitives," insights usually occur randomly, so that the protocol for testing would have to accommodate this unpredictability of performance.

In the 1980s, scientists made an extensive study of mathematically and verbally gifted children, deriving from this study the hypothesis that there are prenatal causes for particular forms of giftedness. Even as I write, scientists are also studying the criminal mind in an attempt to learn what chemical imbalances, what possible structural anomalies, might account for the markedly deviant behavior of criminals.

Why, then, isn't someone looking for biological links in the case of the psychically gifted? Why is it that scientific curiosity has run out just as the mind game is beginning to get interesting?

Since there are four major disciplines upon which the subject of *psi* seems to impinge, I decided to select at random a psychiatrist, an anthropologist, a neurosurgeon and a theologian, in order to elicit their views and their opinions on this subject.

I first contacted a widely traveled anthropologist who lived in Vermont. In speaking with her, I found that she apparently had no quarrel with the idea of the psychic gift, and regarded its acceptance or rejection as dependent on the culture in which it was found.

She explained, "Members of one society may find their psychics comforting, while those of another may view them with alarm. Moreover, the psychics themselves will differ in their demonstrations and interpretations, depending on their particular culture or their particular experience." We both sadly agreed that any gift so randomly demonstrated and so inexact opened the door for a never-ending hoard of frauds—innocent or otherwise—to becloud and demean the very idea itself.

I asked her if she thought that, from an anthropological point of view, the brain of a psychic might differ physically from the brain of a non-psychic. She answered that she "somehow wouldn't think so. I would imagine rather that a 'sensitive' simply has access to her own subconscious, and that to some degree this is possible for us all." By way of analogy, the anthropologist cited the words of her friend the late anthropologist Margaret Mead, who had drawn a fine line between illiterate and preliterate peoples in explaining that the latter had all the potential for literacy and needed only to be taught.

I talked next to a young psychiatrist who was well-known for his success in treating multiple personality disorder and helping those with schizophrenia.

This psychiatrist was able to recall certain patients who, along with whatever mental illness they were suffering from, also claimed to be clairvoyant. He stated, "So far, I have yet to find a claim which I can verify. Rather, I feel that in those I have seen who profess to have this gift the claim itself represents a need to feel 'important,' a way of transcending early childhood trauma."

This professional did not rule out completely the possibility of the existence of a psychic gift; but he affirmed that he personally had seen no proof, and he insisted that those people who claimed to have it whom he had treated professionally were unconsciously compensating for a lack of ego-fulfillment.

More encouraging was the letter I received from a highly respected Baltimore neurosurgeon who, learning of my interest, recalled the following case of one of his patients for me:

"Time blurs some of the details, but I will try briefly to outline my experience as I remember it. About five or six years ago a man was sent to me in consultation with a lower back disorder and I admitted him to the hospital for work-up and surgery. Everything went well and while he was recuperating he said he would like to entertain me since I'd done such a 'good job.' He asked me whether I could remember the name of my first girlfriend, a girl I knew some forty years ago in a city seven or eight hundred miles distant from here. He then wrote her name and gave it to me on a piece of paper. I was stunned. I ran out in the hall and found another doctor and called him in to confirm this exciting feat of mind-reading. He asked the doctor to write down three digits on a piece of paper and, with his back turned, called them out accurately. Later, he produced facts out of the past lives of many of the employees who worked on the floor and had contact with him. In each case, the effect was quite stunning.

"Some days later, he took me aside and told me that I was going to operate the next day at Johns Hopkins Hospital and perform surgery on a child with a brain tumor that would unfortunately turn out to be malignant. He even told me the name of the child, although he got one letter wrong. Interestingly, the tumor was read out by the pathology department as being malignant, but

217

later—after the slides had been sent to the Armed Forces Institute of Pathology—it proved to be benign and I've followed this child over the years. There has been no evidence of reoccurrence.

"On yet another day, I had been bothered by a peculiar pain and was fearful that it might be an indication of cancer. I had a lifelong cancer phobia, which I had pretty well kept to myself. When I made the rounds that particular evening he asked his guests to excuse themselves, put his hands on my shoulders, and said, 'You don't have cancer, stop worrying. You aren't destined to die of it.' Now I must say, parenthetically, that I really never was convinced that he was able to read the future, particularly since on a couple of occasions his predictions did not prove to be totally accurate. I have the suspicion that people with mind-reading abilities become so impressed with their powers that they adopt the gift of prophecy even when they don't deserve it. Although quantum mechanics and other scientific ruminations suggest that the past, present, and future may exist simultaneously in a different part of the space-time continuum, I really don't think there has been any proof of this and I have not yet been convinced in my own mind that prophecy is possible.

"As to his unusual powers, he told me that he did not always possess them. He had apparently been completely average as far as extrasensory perception is concerned until, while in the Far East with his wife, he came down with an illness which must have been some sort of viral encephalitis because he lay in a coma for several days. When he started coming out of the coma, he babbled a great deal. His wife, who was at his bedside, listened to some of the things he was saying and suddenly realized his ravings were actually answering her thoughts. She became so excited by this that she called a physician who came over to try to calm her down. The physician thought that she had been under too much stress and needed a good night's sleep and that she was merely imagining that her husband possessed this unusual ability. At that point he sat up and told the doctor the name of the patient he was going to visit next and the place where the person lived. From then on he had the gift of mind-reading, and apparently it never abated. He certainly demonstrated it to the complete satisfaction of all the people at the hospital who came in contact with him on many occasions.

"Interestingly, when he asked me about the results of his own operation and I responded, 'You tell me,' he indicated that he was unable to do so and that he had great difficulty in reading thoughts of others which concerned himself, his condition or any personal matters of this nature."

The theologian with whom I spoke confessed to having a genuine interest in the subject of *psi*, and said he believed the psychic gift could be a positive influence on the spiritual lives of those who possessed it—if they stayed oriented in this world and if they realized this is the place where they must work and live. "On the other hand," he warned, "in conjunction with an unstable personality, the gift can be distressing, even dangerous, to say nothing of the opportunities this field offers for the fraudulent to take advantage of the gullible. Then there are certain poor benighted souls who apparently have a need to feel interestingly different and, lacking demonstrable skills, home in on one that is hard to assess. None of these considerations, however, take away from the fact that there are some few rare individuals with genuine psychic powers."

Any other group of four respected authorities from these four disciplines might have come up with totally different comments, and it is unlikely there would ever be a consensus among the members of any group of four. Imagine a discussion taking place between a psychoanalyst and a Catholic priest about the revelations of St. John the Divine—or about Joan of Arc and her voices. First, Joan was burned at the stake; and later, she was sanctified! The psychic gift appears to consistently confuse the non-psychic, no matter the weight of intellect or the direction of training brought to bear.

If we agree that man is continually evolving, and that survival is the "name of the game," then we must admit that we have arrived in our present state at a dangerous impasse. We have learned to exploit our planet—almost beyond repair. We have learned to develop weapons—which threaten our survival as a species. If we agree that change is a part of life itself, then we must hope that man will evolve into a higher state in time to save the human race.

We seem to be rapidly approaching an era when we will be capable of directing our own future evolution. Shouldn't we recognize that the ability to read minds, the ability to see the past and predict the future, and the ability mentally to heal the sick, are gifts to be protected and cultivated in the hope that they will appear more frequently among us? Surely, beings possessing six senses are more highly evolved than those possessing only five.

Do we dare to ignore gifts that may herald the arrival of a higher species?

EPILOGUE

The Catholic Church eventually pardoned Galileo.

The British Academy of Science eventually acknowledged the platypus.

Perhaps, if we're patient, there's still a chance for *psi*.

ABOUT THE AUTHOR

Virginia Adair was born and grew up in Atlanta, Georgia, and attended college in Virginia. For many years, she has pursued a career as a portrait painter. Her works are in institutions and in private collections both in America and in Europe. Ms. Adair is also the author of *Eighteenth Century Pastel Portraits* (John Gifford Ltd., 1971). She currently lives in Atlanta.

Index